Symbols of You

A Self-Discovery Reference Guide

Linda Mackenzie

Creative Health & Spirit
Manhattan Beach, CA

Creative Health & Spirit
P.O. Box 385
Manhattan Beach, CA 90267
www.lindamackenzie.net

Copyright © 2022 Linda Mackenzie

All rights reserved. No part of this book may be reproduced or utilized in any form or by any means, electronic or mechanical, including photocopying, recording or by any information storage and retrieval system, without permission in writing from the publisher.

This publication contains the opinions and ideas of the author. It is intended to provide helpful and informative material on the subjects addressed in this publication. It is provided with the understanding that the author and the publisher are not engaged in rendering or giving medical, health, psychological or other professional advice or services in the book. If the reader requires personal medical, health, psychological or other advice a competent professional should be contacted. The author and publisher specifically disclaim all responsibility for any liability, risk, loss, personal or otherwise, that is incurred by the consequence, indirectly or directly, of the use of the applications of this publication.

Library of Congress Control Number: 2022920732
Symbols of You - A Self-Discovery Reference Guide/ by Linda Mackenzie
1. Self Help 2. Reference 3. Spirituality 4. Philosophy 5. New Age I. Title

ISBN 979-8-9867179-0-6 (Print)
ISBN 979-8-9867179-1-3 (Ebook)

Printed in the United States

Book design: Clarity Designworks

To send correspondence to the author of this book, mail a first class letter to the author c/o Publisher. Author will be forwarded your letter or contact the author directly at lindamackenzie.com.

Symbols of You is an amazing collection of knowledge and wisdom. Everyone should have a copy to consult with and learn from. As a physician working with cancer patients, and others, to help them overcome the negative messages they received from health care professionals and others. I know what we can achieve when we connect with our true self and healing ability. This book is a guide book to life. So read and learn.
— BERNIE SIEGEL, MD author of *Love, Medicine & Miracles* and *The Art of Healing*

Knowledge is the key to unlocking the great potential for growth and understanding. Through this book, Linda does an incredible job handing you those keys.
— EMILY A. FRANCIS author of *The Body Heals Itself*

Linda Mackenzie is a wise and insightful spiritual guide who takes us on a holy inner journey to self-revelation. In this fascinating and challenging book, not only do we learn the historical context of the symbols, talisman, and totems of our world's religions, faith communities, tribes, and cultures, but we are given a directional map into our own hearts and souls that enlightens and enriches.
— RABBI WAYNE DOSICK, PH.D. author of *The Real Name of God* and *Radical Loving*

Linda's work pulls back the covers on the fact that we live in the world whose invisible relationships far outweigh those we see, and by which we measure our lives; in so doing, she not only invites readers to examine their consciousness through a much wider lens, but provides them the means to do just that. Well done!
— GUY FINLEY author of *The Secret of Letting Go*

In her newest book, *Symbols of You*, Linda gives you a personal manual to self awareness so you can better understand yourself and what motivates you. Most essentially, by decoding one's spiritual symbols you can see how the Universe supports you. It helps you learn how to decipher the code of mystery in order to direct the course of your life. It is a must read for everyone looking to actualize their truest potential.
— DR. JANE GREER, author *Am I Lying To Myself*

Symbols of You is a compendium of different esoteric knowledge from so many sources, it's like an encyclopedia of mystic information condensed into one user friendly book. You can travel all over the world in this one volume and find symbols that resonate with you. With exercises, visualizations and other tools to enhance consciousness and wellness, this book is a must! It's a Magical Mystical Tour of Symbols!
— ANDI & JONATHAN GOLDMAN, authors, *The Humming Effect* and *Chakra Frequencies*

Other Books by *Linda Mackenzie*

Inner Insights – The Book of Charts
How to Self-Publish & Market Your Personal Growth Book
Help Yourself Heal with Self-Hypnosis

Audios by *Linda Mackenzie*

Total Mind-Body-Spirit Weight Loss Program
Help Yourself Heal – Menopause

Videos by *Linda Mackenzie*

Many Faces of Psychic Ability

Acknowledgements

I wish to express my heartfelt appreciation to all who have loved and supported me during this book creation process. Special thanks goes to:

My family. Lisa and Jack Reitinger - for putting up with and loving me unconditionally. My grandson Cooper Reitinger - who gives me hope for a future that is bigger, better and brighter.

My close circle of friends. Jay Cruz - voice of reason and conjecture. Carolyn McFadden - for giving me wisdom and laughter. Brook Dryden - for helping keep my feet on the ground. Brenda Barnes - for keeping me on my toes. Debi Smith Anderson - for always being in my corner and Barbara Southworth - who although now on the other side still supports and guides me - especially with those pesky computer problems.

My book mentors. Devra Jacobs - for immeasurable advice, book industry wisdom and friendship. Carla Green - for making the manuscript and book cover into a beautiful masterpiece.

It is also with respect and gratitude that I acknowledge the ancient publications, storytellers and philosophers throughout the centuries that have contributed to the extensive research of this book.

Most of all I acknowledge God, the Source, who has guided and given me many gifts to help support people in finding truth and their path to consciousness. I feel deeply grateful and am blessed to be of service.

....

Dedication

I would like to devote this book to all truth seekers looking towards self-discovery and empowerment through connection with Ancient Wisdom. By knowing themselves, these truth seekers expand the level of consciousness which not only embraces the positive aspects in their own life, but expands out to all Consciousness. Therefore the truth seeker, becomes part of the Universal solution to help actualize the positive for the greater good of all.

What better dedication could there be but to you my reader, my treasured truth seeker. This book is dedicated to you.

Table of Contents

Chapter 1	Selecting Your Symbols	1
Chapter 2	Angels	3
Chapter 3	Animals	8
Chapter 4	Archetypes	10
Chapter 5	Aromatherapy	12
Chapter 6	Astrology	14
Chapter 7	Auras	17
Chapter 8	Bach Flower Essences	19
Chapter 9	Birds	21
Chapter 10	Candles	23
Chapter 11	Chakras	25
Chapter 12	Colors	30
Chapter 13	Crystals &Gemstones	36
Chapter 14	Fish	41
Chapter 15	Flowers	43
Chapter 16	Gods & Goddesses	46
Chapter 17	Native American Animal Spirit Guides	51
Chapter 18	Numbers	55
Chapter 19	Numerology	58
Chapter 20	Oriental Horoscope	63
Chapter 21	Palm Reading	66
Chapter 22	Phrenology	70

Chapter 23	Planets	74
Chapter 24	Playing Cards	78
Chapter 25	Shapes, Geometric	83
Chapter 26	Tarot Cards	85
Chapter 27	Tea Leaf Reading	88
Chapter 28	Trees	90
Chapter 29	Water	92

BONUS: HEALTH & AWARENESS CHARTS 95

Chapter 30	Acupressure Points & Application	97
Chapter 31	Cabala (Kabala, Kabbalah)	102
Chapter 32	Cheyenne Medicine Wheel	105
Chapter 33	Chinese Elements	108
Chapter 34	Chinese Herbs	110
Chapter 35	Dice Fortune Telling	113
Chapter 36	Domino Fortune Telling	115
Chapter 37	Herbs	118
Chapter 38	I Ching & Ching Trigrams	121
Chapter 39	Reflexology	126
Chapter 40	Runes	129
Chapter 41	Sioux Four Directions	132
Chapter 42	Vitamins, Minerals, Dietary Supplements	134
Chapter 43	Western Elements	139

Fill-In Charts 141

Introduction

You are special. In fact, each and every person is special and unique. Since everything is connected in a Divine Plan, you are part of that plan. Every individual contributes and has an impact on everything around them. Even if you choose not to take an action, this still produces a reaction on the things around you.

You also have your own individual path in the Divine Plan on which you take your journey through life. The ways in which you experience life, health, and even spirituality on this path are unique to you. Part of your mission on this journey is to find out about you, so you can go beyond your ego to become a more positive force for the greater good of all. Your life's journey is filled with choices of free will and you alone are responsible for every choice you make. Knowing your symbols can help you make more positive choices.

Your self-discovery and growth begins at birth. It continues until you pass over, and, perhaps, even beyond that point. As each step of your growth is accomplished, you receive the knowledge, self-discovery and empowerment to prepare you for your next step. Finding out about yourself is an intricate part of your growth process.

My goal with this book is to help jumpstart your growth process to make your life's journey a happier, healthier and more profound experience. The information in this book is timeless, so after you discover your symbols, you can continue to use this as an ongoing reference book.

If you disagree with some of the symbol meanings in this book, use your gut feel or intuition and interpret the symbols in your own way. You can't make a mistake. This is your life, your growth process and it is exactly right for you whatever you do - so have fun with it!

Love & Light,
Linda Mackenzie

Selecting Your Symbols

You are about to embark on an adventure to find out about YOU! Mankind has used symbols since the beginning of time to help interpret themselves and the world around them. Every symbol can act as a clue to discover who you are. When you interpret a symbol it can show you how your mind thinks or what your body physically needs. It can help you maintain, alter or expand your belief system. Discovering who you are helps you understand yourself, others, life, the world, the universe and spirituality.

Using symbols as guides can give you a faster way of approaching your personal and spiritual growth. Symbols set the stage for increased awareness and active participation in life. They can be touchstones of truth or even protection. Using symbols help you increase your intuition to interpret life and events around you. Symbols just make life more fun.

Everything you come in contact with in your life, or even in your dreams, can act as a symbol. You are the only one who can determine a symbol meaning since no one has lived your life exactly the same way. Your symbols are as unique as you are.

Your brain is divided into two parts: the conscious, left logical side where logic, words and rational thought reside, and the subconscious, right creative side which holds your imagination and intuition. Your symbol selections will probably be based on a combination of thought from both sides of your brain, your unique life experiences and your feelings.

Symbols can be common, universal, or unique. A *common symbol* can be taken from the things you see around you or something you dream about. A *universal symbol* is one whose meanings are generic and well-known and a *unique symbol* is one that has meaning for you.

Some symbols will always be a part of your life and sometimes your symbols may change. Symbols can even have more than one meaning. There is no right or wrong way on how to select your symbols or their interpretation — it is always right for you — at that time. This book provides you with a plethora of symbols comprised from many sources, both past and present. It is designed to be an adventure into your own self-discovery.

Filled with information and symbol charts you can select the symbols that are right for you, but don't limit your symbols to just this book. The more you work with symbols the more apparent they will become to you. You will be able to expand and interpret symbols anytime, anywhere in your every day life. Imagine using symbols and creativity to make your life as interesting as possible in every moment!

In the *Symbols of You* chapters sometimes your symbols will be evident, in others the Discovery exercises and visualizations will help you select your symbol. If for any reason you can't decide which symbol is yours, use your intuition and gut feel. Usually your first feeling is correct. If you disagree with some of the symbol meanings, interpret the symbols in your own way. You can't make a mistake.

You do not have to do the chapters in order. You can do what you like, when you like. In the back of the book there are *fill-in* worksheets so that you can record of all your personal symbols. The fill-in worksheet gives you a written record so you can review your symbols whenever you like.

To successfully use this book there is one important factor to remember — Have Fun!

Angels

An angel is a "pure and divine spirit," a "messenger," a "ministering or guiding spirit" and according to Scriptures employed by God. All religions believe in angels and angels can give us comfort and hope.

The Angel Hierarchy is a division of three groups of angels in order of power, rank and class. The nine Angelic Choirs represent groups of angels in Divine service to God. There are also angels of the zodiac, months, days, and elements. Many of the angels have certain attributes and specialties. You always have more than one angel ready and willing to help you.

ANGEL HIERARCHY

Hierarchy 1	Seraphim - Choir 1		Cherubim - Choir 2		Thrones - Choir 3	
Spirits of:	Love & Positive Universe		Harmony & Wisdom		Will & Justice	
	Michael	Seraphiel	Gabriel	Raphael	Orifiel	Raziel
	Kemeul	Uriel	Cherubiel	Zophiel	Baradiel	Japhakiel
	Jehoel	Metatron	Ophaniel		Zaphkiel	
	Nathaniel					
Residence:	Closest to God		Fixed Stars		Saturn	

Hierarchy 2	Dominions - Choir 1		Virtues - Choir 2		Powers - Choir 3	
Spirits of:	Wisdom & Intuition		Choice & Movement		Form & Space	
	Zadkiel		Uzziel	Haniel	Raphael	
	Muriel		Michael	Babiel	Camael	
	Hasmael		Peuel	Gabriel	Verchiel	
	Zacharel		Tarshiel			
Residence:	Jupiter		Mars		Sun	

Hierarchy 3	Principalities - Choir 1		Archangels - Choir 2		Angels - Choir 3
Spirits of:	Personality & Time		Fire & Ruling Angels		Nature & Messengers
	Uriel	Anael	Gabriel	Raphael	Multitudes of Angels that are intermediaries between God and humans.
	Michael	Raguel	Michael	Remiel	
	Raphael	Gabriel	Uriel	Raguel	
	Remiel		Sariel		
Residence:	Venus		Mercury		Moon

Guardian angels are the guardian spirits of human beings. Everyone has one or more guardian angels that are assigned to them at birth for their protection. The guardian angels may or may not be part of the hierarchy or choirs of angels.

Many angels will come in and out of your life as you need them. After you select your angel's name you can use your angel for special help in their area of expertise. Their area of expertise can be found on the *'Spirits of'* line in the chart. The angels live or have residence on different planets and stars and these areas in which they reside are also given in the chart.

DISCOVERY 1

Selecting Your Angel Symbols

Look at the angel hierarchy and pick an angel's name from each of the nine choirs. Sometimes an angel's name will jump out at you. If not, look at the angel's name and say each one out loud. Pause for a moment after each name and see how it feels to you. Select the angel's name that seems right for you.

In the last choir there are multitudes of angel names. To find your specific angel's name do this simple exercise:

Find a comfortable place where you won't be distracted. Sit in a very comfortable chair with your arms and legs uncrossed. State your intention out loud that you would like to know your angel's name. Close your eyes and begin to quiet your mind. Just concentrate on your breath and breathing. Let any distracting thought just drift away until your mind is quiet. Listen for or see your angel's name appear before you. Whatever name you hear or visualize will be the right one for you.

ZODIAC ANGELS

Zodiac angels rule the twelve signs of the zodiac.

Zodiac Sign	Angel	Zodiac Sign	Angel
Aries	Machadiel	Libra	Uriel
Taurus	Asmodel	Scorpio	Barbiel
Gemini	Ambriel	Sagittarius	Adnachiel
Cancer	Muriel	Capricorn	Hanael
Leo	Verchiel	Aquarius	Gabriel
Virgo	Hamaliel	Pisces	Barchiel

~ ANGELS ~

DISCOVERY 2

Selecting Your Zodiac Angel Symbols

If you know your astrological or zodiac sign, find your angel in the chart. If you do not know your astrological sign, look it up in the astrology chapter and then refer back to this chart.

ANGELS OF THE MONTH

Angels of the months are in charge of ruling the duties involved with the months of the year.

Month	Angel	Month	Angel
January	Gabriel	July	Verchiel
February	Barchiel	August	Hamaliel
March	Machidiel	September	Uriel
April	Asmodel	October	Barbiel
May	Ambriel	November	Adnachiel
June	Muriel	December	Hanael

DISCOVERY 3

Selecting Your Monthly Angel Symbol

Take the month you were born and select the appropriate angel from the chart. These angels can also be called upon for help in association with the particular month they rule.

ARCHANGEL & ANGELS OF THE SEVEN DAYS

Angels of the seven days are in charge of ruling the duties involved with the days of the week.

Day	Archangel	Angel
Sunday	Raphael	Michael
Monday	Gabriel	Gabriel
Tuesday	Khamael	Zamuel
Wednesday	Michael	Raphael
Thursday	Tzaphiel	Sachiel
Friday	Haniel	Anael
Saturday	Tzaphiel	Cassiel

DISCOVERY 4

Selecting Your Archangel Angel & Angel of the Seven Days Symbol

Take the day you were born and select the appropriate archangel and angel from the chart. These archangels and angels can also be called upon for help in association with the particular day they rule.

ELEMENT ANGELS

Elements are the forces of nature that can be expressed as the primary influence of life forces. Western philosophy has four elements and Eastern philosophy has five. Western philosophy associates angels to the four elements.

Element	Angel
Fire	Nathaniel
Air	Cherub
Water	Tharsis
Earth	Ariel

DISCOVERY 5

Selecting Your Element Angel Symbol

To find your element angel, look up your astrological sign in the astrology chapter. Then locate your astrological element and refer back to this chart.

Angel Attributes & Specialties

Angels have certain attributes and specialties that may be able to help you in your time of need. These angels are available to help you with particular problems.

DISCOVERY 6

Getting Help from a Specific Angel

Look at the chart and feel free to pray or ask for a specific angel's help whenever you need it.

~ ANGELS ~

SPECIALTY ANGELS

Specialty	Angel	Specialty	Angel
Aspiration	Gabriel	Judgment	Gabriel
Balance	Michael	Kindness	Rhamiel
Beasts (Tame)	Hariel	Knowledge	Raphael
Beasts (Wild)	Thuriel	Love	Uriel, Theliel, Seraphiel
Benevolence	Zadkiel	Mankind	Metatron
Birds	Arael	Mathematics	Camael
Chance	Uriel	Mediator	Kemeul
Comfort	Gabriel	Memory	Zadkiel
Compassion	Raphael	Mercy	Michael, Rhamiel
Conception	Laila	Morals	Mehabiah
Courage	Babiel	Mountains	Rampel
Daylight	Samshiel	Movement	Peliel
Death	Azrael	Music	Israfil
Destiny	Oriel	Patience	Achaiah
Divination	Eistibus	Personality	Uriel
Dreams	Gabriel	Poetry	Uriel
Earthquakes	Rashiel	Prays for Souls	Sansasiel
Fate	Manu	Progress	Raphael
Fire	Nathaniel	Protection	Camael, Verchiel, Sariel
Fish	Gagiel	Purity	Tahariel
Food	Manna	Revelation	Gabriel
Forests	Zuphlas	Righteousness	Michael
Forgetfulness	Poteh	Science	Raphael
Free Will	Tabris	Sea	Tamiel, Rampel
Future	Isiaiel	Sky	Sahaqiel
Grace	Anachel. Haniel	Solitude	Cassiel
Harmony	Ophaniel, Zophel	Strength	Michael, Zeruch
Healing	Raphael	Thunder	Uriel
Hidden Things	Nathanael	Time	Raguel
Holy Spirit	Gabriel	Trees	Maktiel
Hope	Phanuel	Trust	Michael
Human Sexuality	Anael	Truth	Michael, Gabriel
Human Stupidity	Peniel	Understanding	Gabriel
Intuition	Hasmal, Muriel	Victory	Bahram
Inventions	Liwet	Will	Razdiel
Joy	Raphael, Cassael	Wisdom	Zadkiel, Zachariel
Justice	Japhkiel, Orifiel	World	Michael, Metatron

Animals

Animals have been a source of fascination to humankind since the beginning of time. They are intelligent, conscious beings that can experience emotions, such as love, joy, and grief. Animals have a way of reflecting the humanity in us all.

According to Native American traditions, if an animal appears in your dreams or crosses your path this has a meaning or message for you. Many Native Americans believe animals act as spirit guides or protective spirits. Sometimes Shamans identify with the attributes and qualities of an animal to alter their state of consciousness.

Animal symbols can give you clues to your subconscious emotions or instincts. They may even represent your survival instinct. However you choose to use your animal symbols is exactly right for you.

DISCOVERY 1

Selecting Your Animal Symbols and Animal Spirit Guide

Look at the chart and pick two animals that seem to resonate with you. If you cannot select one think about each animal and how it relates to you and then select the ones you want. To find out about what animal is your animal spirit guide do this simple exercise. If you discovered your animal spirit guide place the information in your fill-in chart. For those of you who did not meet your animal spirit guide in this exercise, try this exercise again or perhaps your animal spirit guide will come to you in a dream. Just be open and eventually your animal spirit guide will come forth.

Visualization
The Green Forest

Find a comfortable place where you won't be distracted. Sit in a very comfortable chair with your arms and legs uncrossed. State your intention out loud that you would like to know your animal spirit guide. Close your eyes and begin to quiet your mind. Just concentrate on your breath and breathing. Let any distracting thought just drift away until your mind is quiet. Now imagine you are in a wonderful green forest. The sun is shining through the green trees and you are sitting on the bank of a winding stream. You feel so calm and relaxed, without a care or worry in the world. As you relax near the stream look to

~ ANIMALS ~

your right. Watch as your animal spirit guide approaches you. Look at the animal's shape and color. As the animal comes closer look in it's eyes. You feel and know that this animal is here to help you. Listen as your animal guide talks to you giving you all the information that you need at this time. When you are done — open your eyes.

ANIMAL SYMBOL CHART

Animal	Meaning	Animal	Meaning
Antelope	Action	Jaguar	Master, Guidance
Armadillo	Defense	Kangaroo	Abundance
Badger	Aggression, Persistence	Lamb	Innocence, Peace
Bat	Intelligence, Rebirth	Leopard	Bravery, Aggression
Bear	Power, Strength	Lion	Justice, Courage
Beaver	Resourceful, Busyness	Lynx	Psychic, Secrets
Big Horn Sheep	Conqueror	Mole	Trust, Sense of Touch
Bobcat	Independence	Monkey	Childishness
Buffalo	Abundance, Mystical	Moose	Balance, Spontaneity
Bull	Sexual Energy, Morality	Mountain Lion	Leader, Personal Power
Camel	Stamina, Dignity	Mouse	Evasive, Busy
Cat	Independence, Guardian	Mule	Stubborn
Cougar	Leadership	Otter	Playful, Quick
Cow	Female Power, Fertility	Panther	Fierceness
Coyote	Cunning, World Order	Pig	Intelligence
Crocodile	Strong Will	Porcupine	Protection
Deer	Loveliness, Renewal	Possum	Avoidance
Dog	Loyalty, Faithfulness	Rabbit	Gentleness, Humility
Dolphin	Community	Raccoon	Enterprising
Donkey	Helpful, Patience	Rat	Survival, Good Luck
Dragon	Spiritual Power	Seal	Playful
Elephant	Strength, Memory	Sheep	Trust, Innocence
Elk	Bravery, Majesty	Skunk	Defense, Protection
Fox	Wily, Cunning	Snake	Raw Energy, Wisdom
Frog	Transformation	Squirrel	Resourcefulness
Gazelle	Innermost Heart	Stag	Regeneration
Goat	Procreation, Vitality	Tiger	Spiritual Exertion
Hare	Intuition, Insight	Tortoise	Long Life
Hedgehog	Protection, Wealth	Turtle	Patience, Good Luck
Hippopotamus	Fertility	Whale	Consciousness
Horse	Energy, Power, Freedom	Wolf	Organization, Family

Archetypes

Carl Jung discovered that using the roles of archetypes and myths as models could further a person's growth and spiritual awareness. Archetypes and myths are representative of human experiences, ideas, and consciousness. The lessons are as valuable today as when they were created. These collective human experiences embrace both the positive and negative aspects of human behavior.

By looking at and identifying with an archetype or myth you may find a solution to a problem, or even find out about your character, strengths, creativity, self-worth, and weaknesses. Archetypes and myths can be used as role models towards taking personal responsibility and gaining self-empowerment to fulfill your goals.

To identify with an archetype or myth you need to know about them. You will recognize many of these myths and archetypes. To find out about the ones you do not recognize I suggest buying a book or going to the library to find out about them.

DISCOVERY 1

Selecting Your Archetype Symbol

Look at the goal column on the chart and select what best characterizes what you are seeking in this time of your life. Transfer that archetype/myth to your fill-in chart. To discover how this can help you reach your goal, research at the library or a respected internet source and read the myth and/or story about the archetype to see how it applies to your life.

~ ARCHETYPES ~

ARCHETYPE CHART

Goal	Archetype	Myth
Abundance	Emperor Empress	King Midas
Creativity	Aphrodite Orpheus Apollo Erato	Icarus & Daedalus
Healing	Hermes Isis	
Inner Peace	Artemis	
Inspiration	Pegasus The Three Greek Muses	
Intuition	Apollo Cassandra Hermes	Pandora's Box
Kindness	Androcles	Androcles & The Lion
Knowledge & Wisdom	A Shaman Guru Sage	Jason & The Golden Fleece
Love	Aphrodite Dionysus Ishtar	Echo & Narcissus Psyche & Eros Lancelot & Guinevere
Relationships	Romeo & Juliet Solomon & Bethsheba	Hera & Zeus Abraham & Sarah
Sacrifice	Prometheus	Abraham & Isaac
Spiritual Fortitude	Joan of Arc Jesus	The Holy Grail
Strength	Hercules Amazons	Richard the Lionhearted
Surrender	Adam Eve	The Illiad
Transformation	Eos Iris	Demeter & Persephone
Warrior Spirit	Ares Athena	

Aromatherapy

The life force or energy of a plant is said to contain it's essential oil. The "aroma" of certain essential plant oils have been used as a "therapy" since before 2000 B.C. Essential oils are odorous and easily evaporate in the open air. The oils are typically extracted from the plant by steam distillation.

Aromatherapy oils can be used as a bath, perfume, massage oil, compress, room freshener or inhalant to produce positive results in emotional and physical symptoms. The action of essential oils is almost immediate and each essential oil has its own therapeutic qualities. Chemical copies, such as those used in perfumes, do not have therapeutic properties. Essential oils need to be treated with knowledge and respect and before use study is recommended.

DISCOVERY 1

Selecting Your Aromatherapy Symbol

If you have experience with essential oils, look at the chart and select the oil you know and like best. If you are new to essential oils, try going to a health food store and smelling the samplers on display. Your sense of smell and your reaction to the oils will tell you which one is right for you.

AROMATHERAPY CHART

Oil	Use	Oil	Use
Aniseed	cramping, digestion, cough	**Lemon**	boils, capillaries, oily skin
Basil	anxiety, nerves, mental fatigue	**Lemongrass**	spiritual protection, acne
Benzoin	urinary infections, skin	**Lime**	oily skin, sun tanning
Bergamot	anxiety, depression, skin	**Mandarin**	digestion
Black Pepper	muscle aches & pains, colds	**Marjoram**	anxiety, stress, headaches, panic attacks, hypertension
Cedar	past emotional pain, oily skin	**Melissa**	headaches, brain fatigue
Chamomile	anger, digestion, insomnia, overwork, PMS, skin	**Myrrh**	spiritual protection, lung disorders, throat/mouth infection
Cinnamon	digestion, respiratory systems	**Neroli**	stress, sadness, insomnia, anxiety, dry skin, depression
Clary Sage	anxiety, depression, laryngitis, throat infection, mental strain, cramps, spiritual purification	**Orange**	digestion, stress
Clove	stimulating, aphrodisiac	**Patchouli**	sensual stimulant, skin
Cypress	varicose veins, hemorrhoids	**Peppermint**	digestion, memory, nausea, congestion, joint pain, muscle pain, mental fatigue
Eucalyptus	colds, congestion, arthritis, infections, muscle pain	**Pine**	respiratory infection, aches, pains, congestion
Evening Primrose Oil	nervous disorders, PMS, circulation, reproduction	**Rose**	stress, anxiety, impatience, confusion, heart sorrow, emotional trauma, skin
Fennel	indigestion, flatulence, diuretic	**Rosemary**	mental fatigue, memory, arthritis, congestion, aches
Frankincense	nightmares, fear, wrinkles	**Rose Otto**	depression, grief, hang over
Geranium	tension, dry or inflamed skin	**Rosewood**	dry skin
Ginger	muscle strains, colds, flu	**Sandalwood**	stress, fear, insecurity,
Grapefruit	resentment, gall/kidney stones	**Tagettes**	spiritual protection
Jasmine	depression, frigidity, PMS, lack of confidence, skin, emotional coldness,	**Tea Tree**	burns, insect bites, ringworm, athletes foot, thrush, warts, herpes, nail infections, colds
Juniper	cystitis, urinary infection, cramps, arthritis, circulation	**Thyme**	muscle strains, aches and pains, infection
Lavender	anxiety, burns, wounds, stress, insect bites, sensual stimulant, skin inflammation, dermatitis	**Ylang Ylang**	depression, anger, frigidity, impotence, hypertension, aphrodisiac, palpitations.

Astrology

Astrology is considered as a science. The basis of astrology is the study of the Zodiac, an imaginary belt in the heavens, and the related positions of the planets, moon, and sun at the time of birth. In essence astrology is the study of time and it's effect on matter and form. Astrology can give you an understanding of yourself and others around you.

Determined by your date and place of birth your astrological sign is categorized as one of the twelve Zodiac signs. Your astrological chart can reveal your character and can tell the story of your life path based upon your characteristics.

Although some of the traits and characteristics you do have will fall into the general category of your astrological sign, remember that not everyone of the same sign is exactly the same. This is because the exact time of your birth determines the exact characteristics that you will have. A complete *natal chart*, based upon the positions of the sun, moon, and planets at the time of your birth can give you complete details of your exact characteristics.

ASTROLOGY SIGN SYMBOLS

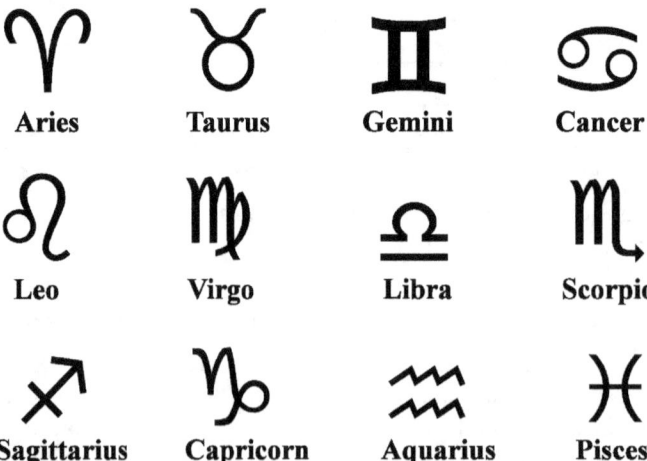

~ ASTROLOGY ~

DISCOVERY 1

Selecting Your Astrology Symbols

Look at Astrology Chart 1 and 2 and select the appropriate information to fill in your chart.

ASTROLOGY CHART 1

Sign	Motto	Symbol	Element	Planet	Colors	Gemstones
Aries 03/21-04/20	I Am	Ram	Fire	Mars	Bright Red	Diamond Garnet Ruby
Taurus 04/21-05/21	I Have	Bull	Earth	Venus	Deep Blue	Emerald Sapphire Rose Quartz
Gemini 05/22-06/21	I Think	Twins	Air	Mercury	Blue	Turquoise Aquamarine Clear Quartz
Cancer 06/22-07/23	I Care	Crab	Water	Moon	Green	Pearl Moonstone Alexandrite
Leo 07/24-08/23	I Protect I Will	Lion	Fire	Sun	Orange Yellow	Tigers Eye Topaz Citrine
Virgo 08/24-09/23	I Analyze I Serve	Virgin Sphinx	Earth	Mercury	Blue	Agate Pink Jasper Amazonite
Libra 09/24-10/23	I Harmonize	Scales	Air	Venus	Pink	Opal Tourmaline Kunzite
Scorpio 10/24-11/22	I Desire	Scorpion Phoenix	Water	Mars Pluto	Red Black	Topaz Garnet Bloodstone
Sagittarius 11/23-12/21	I Seek I See	Archer Centaur	Fire	Jupiter	Indigo Violet	Turquoise Lapis Lazuli
Capricorn 12/22-01/20	I Use	Goat	Earth	Saturn	Black Green	Onyx Malachite
Aquarius 01/21-02/19	I Know I Differ	Water Bearer	Air	Uranus Saturn	Electric Blue	Sapphire Aquamarine
Pisces 02/20-03/20	I Believe	Fish	Water	Neptune Jupiter	Deep Purple	Amethyst

ASTROLOGY CHART 2

Sign	Body Part	Musical Note	Number	Archetype	Compatibility
Aries 03/21-04/20	Head	C	9	Hercules Athena	Aries, Leo, Libra Sagittarius
Taurus 04/21-05/21	Throat Neck	C Sharp D Flat	6	King Minos Aphrodite	Taurus, Cancer, Leo, Scorpio, Pisces, Capricorn
Gemini 05/22-06/21	Shoulders Arms Lungs	D	5	Hermes Dioscuri	Aries, Libra, Sagittarius
Cancer 06/22-07/23	Stomach	D Sharp E Flat	2, 7	Medusa Orpheus	Taurus, Cancer, Virgo, Scorpio, Pisces, Capricorn
Leo 07/24-08/23	Heart Back Solar Plexus	E	1, 4	Apollo Penelope	Aries, Libra, Taurus, Aquarius
Virgo 08/24-09/23	Intestines	F	5	Isis Merlin	Taurus, Cancer, Virgo, Pisces, Capricorn
Libra 09/24-10/23	Kidneys	F Sharp G Flat	6	Aphrodite Odysseus	Aries, Libra, Leo, Sagittarius, Capricorn
Scorpio 10/24-11/22	Sexual Organs	G	9	Persephone Gilgamesh	Taurus, Cancer, Scorpio, Pisces, Capricorn
Sagittarius 11/23-12/21	Thighs	G Sharp A Flat	3	Hercules Zeus	Aries, Gemini, Leo, Aquarius, Sagittarius
Capricorn 12/22-01/20	Knees Bones	A	8	King Midas Pan	Taurus, Cancer, Leo, Scorpio, Virgo, Pisces
Aquarius 01/21-02/19	Nervous & Circulatory Systems	A Sharp B Flat	4, 1	Atlanta Peter Pan	Aries, Gemini, Leo, Aquarius, Libra Sagittarius,
Pisces 02/20-03/20	Feet	B	3	Dionysus Teresa of Avila	Taurus, Cancer, Scorpio, Virgo, Leo, Capricorn

Auras

Auras are atmospheres of energy that arise and surround the body. This auric field, or magnetic force field, around the body is constantly changing. The mind-body-spirit of an individual is reflected in the aura. Auras can show everything that a person was, is, or will be.

Impressions, feelings, thoughts, words. and actions are registered in a person's aura.

Auras present themselves in colors. These colors vary and are constantly changing. Being consciously aware can change the size of your aura and is directly related to an individual's spiritual growth. The object of knowing about, or seeing your aura, can help you understand yourself and others around you.

The chart depicts the different auric bodies and their attributes. Since your aura is constantly changing, so will your colors. This chart is for information purposes.

If you can detect your own or someone else's aura you are very lucky because not all people can see auras. Here is a visualization and a practice to help you discover your aura.

Open Eye Visualization
Seeing Your Aura Colors

Start to breathe in and out deeply. Now focus on your breath and breathing. Get very relaxed. Hold out your arm against a solid white wall, squint your eyes and look at the outside of your arm. Concentrate and keep looking at the outside of your arm against the white wall. At first you may see an outline around your arm, similar to heat waves off of a hot pavement. Concentrate and look closer at this outline. Explore the energy around your arm and see if you can spot any of your aura colors.

If this doesn't seem to work, try placing your arm against a very dark, solid surface and do the exercise again. If you still don't see it, be patient and keep trying and eventually you will find your aura.

AURAS

Body	Base	Energy Qualities	Hue Qualities	Sound	Feeling	Phrase
1st Physical	Experience, Sensation	Physical Matter	Physical Body	Normal Sounds	Consciousness	I Exist
2nd Etheric	Karma, Love, Astrological	Physical Sensation	Pale Shining Blue	Keen Hearing	Deep Physical Experience	I Respond
3rd Mental	Rational thought, Mental process	Partitioned Planes	Yellow Light	Rhythmic Beat	Logical Unattached Experiences	I Think
4th Astral	Desire, Emotional thought Out of body	Timeless, Sensitivity, Change	Red, Opaque multicolor	None	Emotional experience, Unity with another	I Blend
5th Higher Mind	Responsibility, Divine will, Holy Spirit, Universal consciousness	Thought focusing, Action of thought	Cobalt blue, Azure, Purple	Voice Within	Awareness Strength Higher force connection	I Will
6th Casual	Wisdom, Higher self, Universal love	Peace, Security	Prismatic pastels with gold and white light, Pink, Electric blue, White	White Noise	Spiritual ecstasy	I Know
7th Ketheric	Body/soul merge Life force, Higher mind, Spiritual strength	Energy source	Gold	Humming	Peace & Security	I Am

Bach Flower Essences

Bach flower essences are holistic remedies for emotional problems, stability, and harmony. They were developed by Dr. Edward Bach in the 1930's. The remedies are comprised of specific non-toxic plant, bush, tree, and flower tinctures which are distilled into a tonic or drops. These drops or tinctures are taken internally to help the body's own systems to fight emotional distress.

The flowers that are used were selected because they plants that embody a certain potential of the Soul. Bach flowers actually acts as a catalyst that helps the Soul reconnect harmoniously to your personality. Thus supporting your personality to find its way back to the harmony.

Bach flower essences are said to transform the body's negative energy into positive energy. The essences work energetically, are self-regulating and produce no side effects. The Bach Flower Remedies tend to communicate information through higher vibrations that stimulate our mental and emotional healing forces, which helps the body's own internal defense systems to fight stress and disease.

DISCOVERY 1

Selecting Your Bach Flower

You can use the special Bach Flowers for different emotional problems as they arise. Take a look at the chart and see if you are currently experiencing one or more of the symptoms. If you are, look at the Bach Flower remedy name and place this information in your fill-in chart.

If you choose to try a Bach Flower remedy, they can usually be found at your local health food store or on the internet.

BACH FLOWERS

Symptom	Root Problem	Bach Flower Remedy	Result
Anguish	Despair	Sweet Chestnut	Optimism
Apathy	Lack of Interest	Wild Rose	Interest
Apprehension	Fear	Aspen	Fearlessness
Deep Gloom	Lack of Interest	Mustard	Serenity
Dislikes Change	Over-Sensitivity	Walnut	Ability to Adjust
Doubt of Own Judgment	Uncertainty	Cerato	Intuition
Easily Discouraged	Uncertainty	Gentian	Perseverance
Envy, Jealousy	Over-Sensitivity	Holly	Tolerance
Exhaustion	Lack of Interest	Olive	Peace of mind
Extreme Fear	Fear	Rock Rose	Heroism
Guilt	Despair	Pine	Balanced Self
Harmful to Self and Others	Fear	Cherry Plum	Mental Control
Hopelessness	Uncertainty	Gorse	Hope
Impatience	Impatience	Impatiens	Understanding
Indecision	Uncertainty	Scleranthus	Balance
Indifference	Lack of Interest	Clematis	Interest
Inferiority	Lack of Confidence	Larch	Confidence
Lack of Direction	Frustration	Wild Oat	Peacefulness
Obsessive Concern	Fear for Others	Red Chestnut	Fearlessness
Over Critical	Over-Caring	Beech	Tolerance
Over Dominance	Arrogance	Vine	Balance
Over Enthusiasm	Over-Caring	Vervain	Calmness
Overwhelmed by Responsibility	Despair	Elm	Confidence
Past Nostalgia	Lack of Interest	Honeysuckle	Letting Go
Preoccupation	Worry	White Chestnut	Stillness
Possessiveness	Over-Caring	Chicory	Selflessness
Pride	Loneliness	Water Violet	Tranquillity
Procrastination	Uncertainty	Hornbeam	Faces Problems
Repeat Mistakes	Lack of Interest	Chestnut Bud	Keen Observation
Resentment	Despair	Willow	Openness
Sad About Illness	Despair	Oak	Courage, Hope
Self-Concern	Loneliness	Heather	Selflessness
Self-Denial	Over-Caring	Rock Water	Enjoyment
Self-Disgust	Despair	Crab Apple	Self Satisfaction
Shyness	Fear of Known Things	Mimulus	Fearlessness
Subservience	Over-Sensitivity	Centaury	Maintain Own Will
Torture Behind Cheerfulness	Over-Sensitivity	Agrimony	Optimism
Trauma	Despair	Star of Bethlehem	Relief

Birds

Birds sometimes represent your spirit of transcendence to your next step in growth. They can also represent your intuition, freedom, a journey, emotional or mental release from a situation, a change or movement in a situation, or a discovery about yourself at your soul level. Birds can also symbolize joy, good news, beauty and love.

The Native Americans believe birds act as messengers and have meanings for you if they appear in your dreams or cross your path. They also believe that birds can act as spirit guides.

To find your bird symbols use one or all of these things:

DISCOVERY 1

Selecting Bird Symbol

Look at the bird names and descriptions on the BIRD CHART that follows. See which birds you are drawn to. Pick two or three birds that seem to resonate with you. If you cannot select one, think about how you feel about each bird and how it relates to you and then select them.

DISCOVERY 2

Dream About Your Bird Symbol

Place a pencil and paper by your bedside. Before you go to sleep, ask for your bird symbols to be shown to you in a dream and that you will remember them when you awaken. When you awaken write down the answers or the birds you remember.

Visualization
The Forest of Trees

Find a comfortable place where you won't be distracted. Sit in a very comfortable chair with your arms and legs uncrossed. State your intention out loud that you would like to know your bird spirit guide. Close your eyes and begin to quiet your mind. Just concentrate on your breath and breathing. Let any distracting thought just drift away until your mind is quiet.

Now imagine you are in the mountains. The sun is shining through a forest of green trees. It is so peaceful here and you feel so calm and relaxed. The air smells soft and sweet. You are sitting on your favorite color blanket. Look up into the trees. Above you is a branch with the most beautiful bird you have ever seen. Look at the bird. See the bird's shape and color. You feel and know that this bird is here to help you. Listen as your bird conveys a message to you. You know it is giving you all the information that you need at this time. Remember this bird and when you are ready — open your eyes.

If you discovered your bird spirit guide place the information in your fill-in chart. For those of you who did not meet your bird spirit guide in this exercise, perhaps your bird spirit guide will come to you when you are walking through nature. Just be open and eventually your animal spirit guide will come forth.

BIRD SYMBOLS

Bird	Meaning	Bird	Meaning
Blue Jay	Adaptability, Survival	Hummingbird	Joy, Bliss
Blackbird	Intelligence	Macaw	Victory, Success
Canary	Joy, Harmony	Ostrich	Justice, Equality
Cardinal	Beauty, Self-Worth	Owl	Wisdom, Truth
Chickadee	Optimism	Peacock	Universal Consciousness
Chicken	Foolishness, Fertility	Pelican	Saver, Self-Sacrifice
Crane	Long Life	Pheasant	Harmony
Crow	Magic, Change	Quail	Family
Dove/Pigeon	Hope, Peace, Love	Raven	Shifting, Healing, Prophecy
Duck, Domestic	Marital Happiness	Robin	New Growth
Duck, Wild	Adventure	Rooster	Honesty, Confidence
Emu	Justice, Truth	Sea Gull	Freedom
Eagle	Power, Endurance	Sparrow	Companionship
Falcon	Strength, Telepathy	Stork	Good Fortune, Philosophy
Flamingo	Grace	Swan	Grace, True Self
Goose, Domestic	Quarrelsome, Fertility	Turkey	Forgetful, Restless
Goose, Snow	Fidelity	Vulture	Fate, Purification
Hawk	Spiritual Awareness, Transformation, All-Seeing	Woodpecker	Resourceful, Repetitive
Heron	Self-Reliance, Long Life	Wren	Adaptability, Rebirth

Candles

Candles are a source of light and beauty. They have been known as symbols of illumination, gentle persistence, and revitalization. The flame of the candle is an ancient symbol for the Light of God and spiritual consciousness, knowledge and awakening.

The original word meaning of candle comes from the Latin word *candere* which means "to shine." The Chinese created candles from whale fat as early as 221 B.C., while the Egyptians formed the beeswax candle in 3000 B.C.

Meditating with candles can help one become calm, focused and balanced. This helps to alleviate stress. Good health, awareness, and sensitivity increases with less stress. Remember fire brings in transformation and change. Fire also cleans, heals and purifies.

Candles of different colors effect the physical, mental, emotional, and spiritual bodies of a person by stimulating the higher frequencies in the brain. Each color has its own unique qualities and vibrational frequencies. These frequencies are released and activated when a candle is lit.

DISCOVERY 1

Selecting & Using Your Candle Color

Look at the CANDLE CHART and select the color candle that best matches what you need to accomplish your goal. Candles can work by just placing them around your rooms. You can also change candle colors and use them as you need to and refer to the CANDLE CHART to help you select the ones that best matches what you want to accomplish whenever you want. In addition to the colors of the candles you choose you can also get an a little extra energy boost to achieve your goal and intentions by trying these additional practices.

DISCOVERY 2

Boosting Energetic Purpose Using Candles

Think about your goal before you select your candle. After selecting the right candle for your purpose light the candle. Get in a comfortable place and place the candle in a safe space in front of you. Become relaxed and clear your mind. State your intention or goal. Now look deep into the candle's fire. Meditate about your goal for as long as you need.

DISCOVERY 3

Using Candle Color and Aromatherapy

By matching specific candle color with a specific scent the door to awareness will be opened even more. Check out the aromatherapy uses in the aromatherapy chart in Chapter 5. Choose a scent and candle color that best fits what you want to accomplish. Try to find your specific candle color and scent in your local store or candle shop and then go to a comfortable place and place the candle in a safe space in front of you. Relax and get centered. State your intention or goal. Look deep into the candle's fire and concentrate on your goal or purpose. Feel the energy. Smell the aroma. Feel, know and trust that your goal is being accomplished. Meditate on the candle for as long as you need.

CANDLE CHART

Candle Color	Meaning
Aquamarine	Peace, Protection
Black	Grounding, State of Grace, Creative Void, Receptivity
Blue	Truth, Fidelity, Healing, Compassion, Spiritual Tranquillity
Brown	Grounding, Focus, Practicality, Sensual Awareness
Green	Healing, Balance, Growth, Abundance, Spiritual Assistance
Gold	Life Force, Vitality, Purity, Enlightenment, Spiritual Strength
Indigo	Vision, Innovation, Clarity, Insight, Invention
Magenta	Intuition, Inspiration, Creativity, Vitality
Orange	Courage, Esteem, Bravery, Pride, Ambition
Pink	Love, Beauty, Emotional Harmony, Tenderness, Joy, Compassion
Purple	Wisdom, Knowledge, Spirituality, Esteem, Quest, Spiritual Growth
Red	Energy, Passion, Loving Nature, Vitality, Sexual Energy, Spiritual Energy
Rose	Mystical Love, Empathy, Safety
Silver	Communication, Illumination, Wealth, Self-Knowledge, Spiritual Protection
Turquoise	Creative Thought, Artistic Creation, Discipline, Personal Truth
Violet	Miracles, Wisdom, Knowledge, Purification, Spiritual Power
White	Purity, Hope, Peace, True Insight, Divinity, Power, Universal Energy, Cleansing, Protection, Perfection
Yellow	Precision, Vision, Clarity, Intelligence, Happiness, Energy

Chakras

Chakras are the body's major esoteric energy centers. There are seven chakra energy centers which are found in specific locations of the body. Though some people believe there are twelve chakra centers. These energy centers are described as whirling wheels of pure energy light. The life force energy of the body flows through the chakra areas and is then redistributed back into the body. The energy is said to influence emotions, health, vitality, thought, creativity, memory, intuition, psychic abilities, and spirituality.

The chakra energy can be "open" or "blocked." If a chakra is open, positive energy flows freely to the emotional and physical bodies. If a chakra is blocked, the life force energy does not flow as freely. A blockage is caused by negative thought and attitude. This negativity affects the health and happiness of an individual. Working with the chakras can provide an understanding of where your energy is blocked and what negative issues may be causing the blockage. When the chakra source of the blockage is discovered, working on the issue that caused the blockage can manifest its' release. Balancing and aligning the chakras can redirect your energy towards self-empowerment and growth. This allows the energy to flow more freely and help you reach your next step on the road to conscious awareness, health, and happiness.

Chakras 1 through 4 integrate one's physical and psychological energies. Chakras 5 through 7 integrate the physical and spiritual soul energies. The 8th through the 12th chakras integrate the spiritual soul energy with spiritual evolution. Whether you want to accomplish physical, emotional, or spiritual improvement, working with your chakras can help you accomplish your goal.

DISCOVERY 1

Working With Your Chakras

There are many ways in which to work with your chakras for self-empowerment and growth. You may choose to work on a physical ailment, an emotional problem, or even try to work on increasing your spiritual awareness. Remember the whole person is always affected on a physical, emotional, and spiritual level with every issue. The charts below represents a sampling of the physical, emotional, and spiritual attributes of the chakras. When you work on one area, take a look at the other charts and see what may also apply to your situation. For intensive study and applications there are many books available. The following exercises will give you a taste of how to work with your chakras.

1. Select an issue or problem.
2. Look at the charts and identify the applicable chakra that correlates closest to your issue.
3. Ask yourself questions as to what the cause of the problem might be.

The following is a list of sample questions that you might ask yourself:

Chakra 1:

Do you have difficulty in balancing your male/female energy? Are you misunderstanding the cause of your aggression? If you are female: Do you have difficulty expressing and receiving your feminine energy? If you are male: Do you have difficulty with expression and reception of your masculine energy? Are you having problems with survival, sexuality, physical energy, or security issues?

Chakra 2:

Do you feel guilt? Do you refuse to forgive yourself or others? Do you have scattered attention and lack focus? Is there an unresolved issue that you need to resolve or know more about? Are your desires in balance with what you need?

Chakra 3:

Do you fear being controlled? Do you fear getting out of control? Are you trying to control? Do you have difficulty in receiving new information? Do you feel worthless? Do you refuse to embrace the current situations happening in your life? Do you have a life purpose? Are you being selfish?

Chakra 4:

Do you feel that responsibility is a burden? Do you have difficulty in responding to the situations and conditions that are happening in your life? Do you lack inner harmony? Do you have compassion for yourself and others? Are you stopping your growth in some way?

Chakra 5:

Are you willful? Do you have difficulty in creating something? Do you lack discipline? Are you holding back in expressing what you are feeling? Are you in complete truth about the situations in your life? Do you need to some form of self-expression?

Chakra 6:

Do you refuse to accept your perceptions of the situation? Are you using your thinking process effectively? Do you have trouble using and trusting your intuition? Do you lack vision? Are you stifling your imagination? Do you believe and use higher intelligence?

Chakra 7:

Are you misusing your thinking powers? Are you using and receiving information properly? Do you have all the information available? Are you stopping your spiritual awareness?

Are you stopping your path to growth and enlightenment?

Don't limit yourself to these suggested questions, if none seem to fit your situation try thinking and asking ones of your own.

DISCOVERY 2

Working With the Chakra Charts

Look at all the physical, mental/emotional, and spiritual CHAKRA CHARTS and write the information on your fill-in sheets.

After reviewing all the charts, think about any questions you may have about your own physical and mental/emotional attributes in relationship to the chakras. You can choose to use the CHAKRA SPIRITUAL ATTRIBUTES CHART with meditation. Look at that chart and select the appropriate color, musical note, sound, and gemstone and if either mentally imagine the tools or physically use these tools in conjunction with your meditation, shifts and answers may come faster. For example, you can place the color or gemstone on the appropriate chakra area or listen to the chakra musical note or sound. Do whatever is appropriate for you, whenever you need to.

CHAKRA PHYSICAL ATTRIBUTES

Chakra	Name	Location	Physiological/ Endocrine System	Energy Imbalance Physical Manifestation
1st Root	Muladhara	Base of Spine	Reproductive/ Gonad	Infertility Sexual Problems
2nd Sacral	Swadhisthana	Spleen or Navel	Genito-Urinary/ Leydig	Kidney Disorders
3rd Solar Plexus	Manipura	Solar Plexus	Digestive/ Adrenal	Stomach Disorders Liver Disorders Pancreas Disorders
4th Heart	Anahata	Center of Chest	Circulatory/ Thymus	Heart Disorders Blood Disorders
5th Throat	Vishudda	Hollow of the Throat	Respiratory/ Thyroid	Lung Disorders Thyroid Disorders Larynx Disorders
6th Third Eye	Ajna	Between and Slightly above the Eyes	Autonomic Nervous System/ Pituitary	Eye Disorders
7th Crown	Sahasrara	Very Top of the Head	Central Nervous System/ Pineal	Nervous Disorders Mental Disorders

CHAKRA MENTAL/EMOTIONAL ATTRIBUTES

Chakra	Qualities	Type Energy	Side of Brain	Experience	Energy Imbalance Emotional Manifestation
1st	Survival, Sexuality, Vitality, Security, Body Energy	Yang/ Male	Left Logical	Kinesthetic, Tactile	Impotence Frigidity Anger Lust Rebellious
2nd	Emotions, Memory, Well-Being, Abundance, Desire	Yang/ Male	Left Logical	Emotional	Guilt Anxiety Hatred Sadness Nervousness Self-Pity Insomnia
3rd	Balance, Intellect, Self-Power, Ambition, Self-Worth, Confidence, Self-Esteem	Yang/ Male	Left Logical	Gut Feeling	Addiction Avarice Greed Cheating Dementia Lying Overweight Depression
4th	Love, Compassion, Growth, Inner Harmony	Yang/ Male	Left Logical	Unconditional Love	Despair Depression Selfishness
5th	Will, Creativity, Discipline, Self-expression, Communication	Yin/ Female	Right Creative		Apathy Bigotry Fatigue Jealousy Stuttering
6th	Intuition, Vision, Imagination, Higher Intelligence	Yin/ Female	Right Creative		Excessive Crying, Doubt Revenge
7th	Enlightenment, Spiritual Awareness, Refinement	Yin/ Female	Right Creative		Fear

CHAKRA SPIRITUAL ATTRIBUTES

Chakra	Spiritual Qualities	Symbol	Color	Sound	Musical Note	Gem Stones
1st	Intuitive Self-Protection	White Elephant White Horse 4 Petal Lotus	Red White Black	Buzz	C, DO	Ruby Obsidian
2nd	Access to Childhood Experiences	6 Petal Lotus	Gold Yellow Purple White	Ear Ringing, Running Water	D, Re	Garnet, Carnelian
3rd	Psychic Feeling	Ram 12 Petal Lotus	Pink Green	Flute	E, Mi	Citrine Tigers Eye
4th	Psychic Healing	Air, Wind, 16 Petal Lotus	Blue Turquoise	Singing Bells, Seashell Roar	F, Fa	Aventurine Rose Quartz Emerald Kunzite
5th	Psychic Hearing	2 Petal Lotus	Indigo Green	Wind, Ocean	G, Sol	Blue Topaz Chrysocolla Turquoise
6th	Psychic Vision	1000 Petal Lotus	White Lavender Magenta Violet	Ohm, Mantra	A, Ti	Amethyst Moonstone Pearl
7th	Prophecy		Gold Purple	Silence	B, DO	Diamond Gold
8th	Spiritual Harmony and Pure Information		Purple			Diamond Silver Gold Platinum
9th	Caretaker of the Planet		Peach Salmon			Blue Diamond
10th	Solar System Astral Energy		Silver			Green Tourmaline
11th	Galaxy Unification		Gold			Yellow Diamond
12th	Universal Spirituality		Pure White			Pink Diamond

Colors

Color is visible, radiant light energy of specific wavelengths divided into a spectrum of seven colors. Since ancient times color has effected humankind. It has been used in customs, religions, superstition, magic, and mythology.

Each color has its' own energy qualities that effect the whole person. The mind begins to interpret and react to color at the time of birth. Inherited from your parents your initial reaction to color takes place through your brain's neurotransmitters and endocrine system. As you grew and came in contact with people and experiences in your life a psychological conditioned response to color developed. This may be also be caused by cultural attitudes, beliefs, superstitions, economic status, or customs. It is interesting to note that as you grow from your life experiences your color preferences usually change.

Physically the body reacts to color. For example, red increase the pulse and respiratory rate, blood pressure rises, the taste buds become sensitive, appetite is stimulated, and the sense of smell heightens. In contrast blue slows the pulse, heart, and respiratory rate, the body temperature is lowered, perspiration decreases, and appetite is reduced. Every color or combination of colors effects the body physically.

When selecting your color symbols remember that your personal preferences are yours alone and may change in time. Color is fun to work with and can help you clarify your emotions, personality, ways of expression, and aid in healing.

DISCOVERY 1

Selecting Your Personality Color

Look at the chart and pick your favorite color then read the meaning to see if it applies to you. If your particular color is not listed, combine the two or three colors that make up your desired color and read those meanings. Fill in your personal symbol chart.

FAVORITE COLOR

Personal Favorite Color	Personality Traits
Red	Outgoing, Assertive, High Vitality, Impulsive, High Sexual Energy, Loving Nature, Optimistic, Complainer
Orange	Good-natured, Friendly, Loyal, Charitable, People Oriented, Swayed by Other People's Opinions
Yellow	Imaginative, Intelligent, Shy, Good Friend, Nervous Energy, Need to Help the World, Aloof, Loner
Green	Social, Upfront, Reputable, Moral, Good Citizen, Balanced, Family Orientated, Competitive
Blue	Introspective, Sensitive, Deliberate, Conservative, Sober, Devoted, Annoyed by Stupidity
Purple	Intelligent, Spiritual, Witty, Observant, Artistic, Creative, Verbose, Vain
Brown	Conscientious, Dependable, Steadfast, Sensual, Down to Earth, Shrewd, Obstinate
Gray	Cautious, Conservative, Composed, Peaceful, Agreeable, Independent,
Black	Worldly, Polite, Conventional, Regal, Dignified, Receptive, Above Average

DISCOVERY 2

Selecting Your Color Symbols

Look at the following chart and pick out two colors that are your favorites in order of importance. Fill in these color symbols on your personal symbol chart.

You can use this practice to help you use a color to attain a specific goal.

1. Look at the qualities of each color on the chart and select a goal from them. Now look at the name of the color associated with your goal.
2. Find a piece of clothing or scarf and wear this color, or find an item of this color and place it in front of you.
3. Look at the aspect column and read the words for your color.
4. Find a comfortable place where you won't be distracted. Sit in a very comfortable chair with your arms and legs uncrossed. Focus on what you want to accomplish by repeating these words in the aspect column for your color. Close your eyes and begin to quiet your mind. Just concentrate on your breath and breathing. Let any distracting thought just drift away until your mind is quiet. Try picturing your color in your mind. Just imagine your color all around you. Feel it go into your body, shifting, changing anything that is stopping you from reaching your goal. Now feel how what you want to be accomplished is happening right now. Feel the power of your color. You feel,

know, and trust that what you want to accomplish is starting to happen right now, in this moment. Concentrate on this positive feeling and when you are ready open your eyes.

5. You may want to keep a symbol of your color with you to remind you of your goal until you attain it.

COLOR SYMBOLS

Color	Aspect	Quality	Chakra	Sephirah	Musical Note
White	Universal Energy, Peace, Purity	Divinity, Spirit, Insight, Protection, Cleansing	7th Crown	The Crown Kether	C, B
Gold	Life Force, Spiritual Strength	Spiritual Vitality, Substance	3rd, 7th Crown		D
Silver	Communication, Enlightenment, Spiritual Truth	Spiritual Protection, Initiation, Wealth	Cord of 7th Crown	Wisdom Chokmah	G Sharp A Flat
Magenta	Intuition, Inspiration	Creativity, Vitality	6th, 7th 3rd Eye Crown		B
Purple	Spiritual Quest, Wisdom, Knowledge	Spiritual Growth, Esteem	6th, 7th 3rd Eye Crown	Foundation Jesod	B
Indigo	Divine Protection, Vision, Innovation	Invention, Clarity, Insight	6th 3rd Eye		B
Blue	Truth, Higher Mind, Spiritual Tranquillity	Healing, Devotion, Perception, Protection	5th, 6th Throat, 3rd Eye	Mercy Chesed	A A Sharp B Flat
Turquoise	Creativity, Thought, Personal Truth	Idealism, Discipline, Artistic Creation	5th Throat		G
Green	Love, Healing, Renewal	Growth, Balance, Abundance,	4th Heart	Victory Netzach	F, F Sharp G Flat
Yellow	Precision, Vision, Happiness	Clarity, Intelligence, Focus, Energy	3rd Solar Plexus	Beauty Tiphereth	E, D Sharp E Flat
Orange	Courage, Esteem, Sociability	Bravery, Pride, Ambition, Security	2nd Spleen	Glory Chod	C Sharp
Red	Energy, Passion, Life Energy	Vitality, Sexuality, Health, Loving Nature	1st Base	Judgment Geburah	C
Pink	Innocence, Beauty, Emotional Balance	Joy, Tenderness, Compassion, Devotion	4th Heart		F, F Sharp G Flat
Brown	Grounding, Sensuality	Practicality, Stability, Physical Satisfaction	3rd Solar Plexus	The Kingdom Malkuth	
Black	Receptivity, Knowledge	Creative Void, Possibility	Any Chakra	Understanding Binah	

~ COLORS ~

Color Healing Chart 1

Since ancient times color has been used in healing. By using specific colored amulets, fetishes, and talismans, medicine men and shamans believed that these items helped the healing process. Sometimes a patient wore clothing or was treated in room or area of a certain color.

Look at the COLOR HEALING CHART 1 and select the right color for your particular use. Fill in your healing color on your personal symbol chart.

Visualization
Color Breathing

Before breakfast or dinner, close your eyes, and concentrate on the breath and breathing deeply. Breathe rhythmically about 12 times per minute. Imagine you are surrounded by white light that is inside and outside your body. Imagine your pre-selected healing color going to the exact place in your body that needs healing. Feel the healing taking place. When you are done surround yourself with pure white light and then open your eyes.

DISCOVERY 3

Using Your Healing Color

Find a piece of clothing, gemstone or scarf of the exact color you need and place this on the appropriate activation center of the body area which you would like healed or try placing the your healing color on the appropriate body trigger points located in the chart.

COLOR HEALING CHART 1

Color	Activates:	Used For:		Trigger Points:
Red	Sensory Nervous System Blood Circulation Sympathetic Nervous System Left Cerebral Brain	Anemia Asthma Bronchitis Constipation	Listlessness Paralysis Pneumonia Endocrine	Upper/Lower Extremities, Abdomen
Yellow	Motor Nerves Muscle Energy Nerve Regeneration Lymphatic System	Arthritis Constipation Diabetes Digestion	Eczema Liver Kidney Depression	Cerebrospinal System, Abdomen, Kidneys, Lungs, Skin, Sex Organs
Orange	Thyroid Pulse Rate Spleen Pancreas	Asthma Colds Gall Stones PMS	Respiratory Rheumatism Tumors Exhaustion	Abdomen
Green	Muscle & Bone Growth Emotional Stability Tissue Growth Tension Relief	Insomnia Exhaustion Ulcers Laryngitis	Heart Back VD Nervousness	Circulatory System, Endocrine System
Blue	Metabolism Bloodstream Balance Mind Relaxation Vitality	Baldness Burns Ulcer Vomiting	Skin Disease Teeth Eye Digestion	Brain, Heart
Indigo	Parathyroid Blood Purification Muscle Tone Hemostatic Agent	Appendicitis Deafness Pneumonia Ear Disease	Mental Nose Eye Throat	Brain, Heart
Violet	Spleen Upper Brain Bones Potassium/Sodium Balance	Concussion Bone Growth Sciatica Nervousness	Bladder Neuralgia Abdomen Tumors	Brain, Heart, Lungs, Neck, Nervous System

~ COLORS ~

Color Healing Chart 2

Radionics is today's color therapy that uses specific colored lights on the body. COLOR HEALING CHART 2 shows the Ancient Pythagoreanism philosophy which believes in the migration of the soul and that numbers are primary elements of the Universe. A part of the Pythagorean theory is that each color is associated with a musical note. Musical notes produce vibrations to the ears. Color produces vibration to the eyes. By applying the appropriate color and sound, it may change a person's emotional state that may aid the physical healing process.

Select your applicable color and place the information on your fill-in chart.

COLOR HEALING CHART 2

Color	Quality	Musical Note	Pythagorean Quality	Vibrations Per Second
Deep Red	Spiritual Illumination	G	Positive Force Uplifting Gratitude	384
Red Orange	The Absolute Creative Force	A	Health Destruction	213
Yellow	Will Power Unity Understanding	B	Plant/Animal Dense Vibration Penetration	240
Yellow Green	Love Chastity	C	Purification	256
Green Blue	Spirit Renewal	D	Vitality	288
Blue Violet	Healing Cleansing	E	Harmony Healing	320
Violet	Spiritual Power	F	Purification Visualization	341

Crystals & Gemstones

Crystals, gemstones, metals, and ores are one of nature's finest gifts to humankind. Ancient civilizations revered and used them for healing, ceremony, ornamentation, meditation, protection, and good luck.

Each stone vibrates its own unique energy. It is said that by wearing or carrying a stone you can enhance your own energy to help you accomplish your goals. A stone's energy can have an effect on emotional, physical, and spiritual issues.

DISCOVERY 1

Selecting Your Crystal Symbols

Selecting crystals, gemstones, metals, and ores for your symbols can be a rewarding experience. The stones may be acquired as a gift or purchased in a rock shop or metaphysical store. One fun way to acquire stones is by exploring nature's environment and finding them in their natural state.

To select a stone you need to use your intuition or gut feel. Whatever stone you are attracted to is usually the right one for you. Don't just look at the beauty of a stone, feel its energy.

Look at the CRYSTAL CHART and select a stone's name that seems right for you.

DISCOVERY 2

Energetic Crystal Selection

To select a stone for you or someone else go to a rock shop or metaphysical store and stand before a group of stones. Close your eyes and pass your hand, with your palm down, over the stones. Relax and feel the energy. Hint: Sometimes there is a warmth emanating from the stone in a particular spot. Reach down and select a stone or open your eyes and take the first stone that you see.

To select a stone for someone else use the procedure as above but when you close your eyes think of the person or silently repeat the person's name and then select a stone.

You can also do the same thing with jewelry that you own. Make sure that the stones are natural or real and not synthetic. Place the jewelry on a table in front of you. Relax and feel the energy.

DISCOVERY 3

Selecting a Crystal for a Specific Purpose

You can select a stone to help you with a specific purpose. Look at the following charts and decide what it is you want to accomplish. Is it a spiritual, emotional, or physical issue? Then look in the appropriate column and select the name of a stone that best fits your needs. Proceed to your rock shop or metaphysical store. Keep the purpose of your goal in mind. Close your eyes and pass your hand, with your palm down, over a group of specific stones. Relax and feel the energy. Select your stone. Once you have selected your stone you can do one of the following:

1. Wear it.
2. Carry it with you.
3. Hold the stone in your hand and meditate. This is a very powerful way to use your stone.
4. Lay down, relax, and place it on a chakra point. Leave it on the chakra point as long as you feel you need to. (See Chapter 11 — Chakras for chakra locations. Hint: If you use a stone based on the chakra color column in the chart, and place it on that specific chakra point it will boost the energy even more. For example: Use a red stone like garnet or ruby on the 1st chakra located at the base of the spine to help you deal with anger.)
5. If your goal is to help a physical problem, place the stone on the area that needs healing.

DISCOVERY 4

Cleansing Your Crystal

Every so often your stones will need to be cleaned so that they can get back their energy. You can do this in a variety of ways:

- Place the stone in sea salt for 24 hours and then rinse with clean water.
- Wash the stone in the ocean and let it dry in the sun.
- Wash the stone in a running stream or brook and then let it dry in the sun.
- Use sage or incense and pass the stone thoroughly through the smoke.
- With the intent in your mind that all negativity will be released, take a deep breath and blow on the stone.

The following charts are in alphabetical order and show only a small portion of what each stone can do. This will give you a start in using and working with your crystal symbols. Don't forget to fill in your personal symbol chart with your stone symbols.

CRYSTAL CHART

Name	Color	Spiritual Energy	Physical Energy	Emotional Energy
Agate	Variegated	Soul & Body Harmony	Upset Stomach	Increase Acceptance
Alabaster	White	Composure	Heart	Forgiveness
Alexandrite	Green to Red-Violet	Manifestation	Nervous System	Joy Self-Esteem
Amber	Golden Yellow, Yellow/Brown	Universal Perfection	Throat Bladder	Aids Choice Clears Negativity
Amethyst	Pale Violet - Deep Purple	Spiritual Awareness	All	Mind Balance Calmness
Angelite	Blue	Spiritual Protection	Infection Inflammation	Awareness Consciousness
Aquamarine	Light Blue to Deep Green	Spiritual Awareness	Thymus Gland	Peace
Azurite	Azure to Dark Blue	Spiritual Cleansing	Spleen	Comfort
Bloodstone	Deep Green with Red	Spiritual Power	Spine	Higher Self Awareness
Calcite	Various	Appreciation Nature, Arts, and Sciences	Infections	Memory
Carnelian	Red to Orange	Spiritual Perception	Liver Lethargy	Focus, Aids Fear, Envy, Rage & Sorrow
Chalcedony	White, Gray, Black, Blue	Maintains Positive Vibrations	Wounds	Repels Negative Energy
Chrysoberyl	Yellow - Green	Increases Spirituality	Incontinence Infections	Personal Power Charity
Chrysocolla	Blue-Green	Increases Love Capacity	Muscles Lungs	Inner Strength Harmony
Chrysophase	Green	Grace	Dexterity Heart	Reduces Inferiority or Superiority
Cinnabar	Brown-Red	Community, Aids Finance and Business	Blood Body Strength	Dignity Vitality Power
Citrine	Yellow	Supports Will Wealth	Digestion Growths	Clarity Growth
Copper	Copper	Magnifies Healing Energy and Intuition	Circulation Bacterial Infection	Cleansing Sexual Desire Vitality
Diamond	White	Love Harmony Innocence Infinity	Poisons Eyes Chemical Imbalance	Bravery Self-Love Trust Relationships
Emerald	Deep Green	Conscience Love Universal Law Aids Legal Affairs	Diabetes Eyes Spine Lungs Heart	Mental Focus Healing Wisdom Prosperity
Flourite	Green, White, Purple	Visionary Insight	Radiation Colds, Flu	Aptitude Discernment
Galena	Silver Gray	Receptivity Perception	Dizziness Throat	Optimism Generosity

CRYSTAL CHART (cont.)

Name	Color	Spiritual Energy	Physical Energy	Emotional Energy
Garnet	Green, Brown, Yellow, Red	Contemplation Past Life Help	Pituitary Heart, Blood	Creativity Balance, Peace
Gold	Gold	Spiritual Protection	Digestion Breathing, All	Actualization Happiness, Wealth
Hematite	Gray-Black	Peace Dissolves Negativity	Leg Cramps Anemia Insomnia	Calmness Focus Mental Skill
Herkimer Diamond	White	Surrender Attunement Clairvoyance Clairaudience	Body Toxins	Actualization Renewal Spontaneity Love
Iron	Gray-Black	Insight, Knowledge Diplomacy	Sore Throat Muscle Atrophy	Mental and Emotional Balance
Jade	Green	Dream Work Tranquillity	Heart, Hair Kidneys	Aids Problems Harmony
Jasper	Red, Green, Blue, Yellow	Long Term Change	All	Energy Self-Reliance
Kunzite	Pale Pink, Lilac	Discipline	Blood	Foundation
Kyanite	Blue with White, Green, Yellow & Pink	Tranquillity Dream Solving	Muscles Adrenals Brain	Perseverance Emotional Blocks
Lapis Lazuli	Deep Blue	Clairvoyance Total Awareness	Throat Eyes Bone Marrow	Calmness Objectivity Clarity
Lead	Gray	Grounding Sports, Music	Indigestion	Aids Lethargy
Lodestone	Gray	Universal Thought	Lungs	Aids New Ideas
Malachite	Light to Dark Green	Transformation, Spiritual Evolution, Heart Consciousness	Radiation Broken Bones Tumors	Emotional Pain Reason Fidelity Clear Path
Marble	Varied	Meditation Clarity, Dream Recall	Bone Marrow Flexibility	Self-Control Common Sense
Moonstone	Milky Opalescence	Intuition Perception Travelers Protection	Eyes Skin Hair Heart	Balance New Starts Positivity Self-Expression
Obsidian	Black	Grounding Protection	All	Shields Negativity
Onyx	Black	Intuitiveness	Infections Feet	Wise Decisions Guidance
Opal	White Refracts All Colors	Psychic Awakening	Vision Kidneys	Action Loyalty
Pearl	White	Sincerity Guidance	Bloating Fertility	Faith, Integrity Charity
Peridot	Light Green	Protection	Intestines Spleen Lungs	Bruised Ego Acceptance in Relationships
Platinum	Steel Gray-White	Psychic Ability Awareness	Pineal Gland Eyes, Digestion	Permanent Relationships, Self-Approval
Pyrite	Brass Yellow	Protection Universal Energy	Bones Lungs	Well-Being Memory

CRYSTAL CHART (cont.)

Name	Color	Spiritual Energy	Physical Energy	Emotional Energy
Quartz	Clear	Universal Energy, Spiritual Communication Light, Love, Harmony	Fevers Kidneys Pain Swollen Glands Thirst	Dispels ALL Negativity, Perspective, Aids Positive Thoughts and Feelings
Rhondonite	Black with Pink & Yellow	Compassion	Respiratory	Love Brotherhood
Rose Quartz	Pink	Love	Stress, Coughs, Kidneys, Adrenals, Reduces Wrinkles	Self-Love Love of Others Heart Sorrow Rids Negativity Aids All Love
Ruby	Red	Truth Love Nobility Wisdom	Blood Sexual Energy Heart	Happiness Knowledge Wealth Aids Distress
Sapphire	Black, Blue, White, Gray	Intuition Beauty	Blood Veins	Joy Soothing Thought
Sardonyx	Banded Red and White	Defense	Bone Marrow	Aids Desire for Causes
Silver	Silver	Clarity Intuition Spiritual Balance	Stress Toxins Hepatits	Strength Eloquence Patience Persistence
Smokey Quartz	Dark Gray- Brown	Spiritual Clarity Grounding Protection	Equilibrium Congestion	Rids Emotional Blocks Clarity Survival Cooperation
Sodalite	Blue-White	Fellowship Universal Knowledge	Metabolism Insomnia Digestion	Rids Confusion Efficiency Companionship True Emotions
Sulphur	Yellow	Dispels Negativity	Infections Tumor	Willfulness Reasoning
Tigers Eye	Golden Brown	Peace Humanity	Eye Throat	Practicality Aids Sadness
Tin	Grayish White	New Starts	Ulsers, Parasites	Clarity Stops Fear
Topaz	Golden Yellow	Confidence Potency	Strength, Brain Disorders	Stamina, Light, Joy
Tourmaline	Green	Visualization	Eyes, Thymus	Compassion Abundance
Turquoise	Sky Blue Apple Green	Consciousness Knowing Understanding	Aids Accidents Cataracts All	Attunement Protection Wisdom
Zircon	Red, Green, Yellow, White, Light Blue	Illumination Union Understanding	Sciatic Nerve Bones Muscles	Virtue Balance Perserverance

Fish

In the past, fish have been used to symbolize renewal, immortality, rebirth, fertility, abundance, life, and spirituality. As your personal symbols fish can symbolize your potential, hidden personality traits or how you are handling a situation in life.

There are many ways in which you can use your fish symbols to increase your self-awareness.

Here are some suggestions to help you discover which fish are your symbols. Don't forget that symbols are for your own self-discovery and however you choose to interpret and use them exactly right for you. You will not find a dolphin or whale with the fish because they are mammals and listed in the animal chart in chapter 3.

DISCOVERY 1

Selecting Your Fish Symbols

To find your fish symbols for your hidden potential and personality traits. Cover up the meanings column on the fish chart with your hand or a piece of paper. Look at the fish names and select four fish that you like or are drawn to. Look at the meanings. Write the meanings down in the order you selected them in your personal symbol fill in chart. The first fish you selected represents your hidden potential. The remaining three fish you selected represent some of your personality traits.

DISCOVERY 2

Using Your Fish Symbol

Try this practice to give you insight into how you are handling a current situation. Think of your current situation. Now cover the meaning column in the fish chart. Select three fish you feel are right or that you are drawn to. Now look at the meanings. 1) The first fish selected represents how you handled the situation in the past. 2) The second fish selected represents how you are presently handling the situation. 3) The third fish selected represents how you might handle the future of the situation.

FISH CHART

Fish Name	Meaning	Fish Name	Meaning
Barnacle	Parasitic	Parrot Fish	Beauty
Barracuda	Patient, Observant	Piranha	Aggressive, Frenzied
Carp	Perseverance	Salmon	Precognition, Procreation
Crab	Renewal, Mediator	Sea Horse	Peaceful, Fatherly Love
Flying Fish	Joy, Uniqueness	Sea Urchin	Latent Power
Grouper	Territorial	Shark	Survival
Jelly Fish	Apprehension, Fear	Shrimp	Social, Domestic
Lobster	Aggressive, Male Energy	Squid	Resistance
Manta Ray	Beauty, Grace	Starfish	Divine Love
Moray Eel	Curiosity	Swordfish	Purity, Supernatural
Octopus	Emotional, Intelligent	Trout	Knowledge, Wisdom
Oyster	Rebirth, Fertility	Tuna	Mobility

Flowers

Flowers have always been appreciated by people. Given at weddings, sick beds, or as gifts, flowers send messages of love, joy, friendship, and fidelity. Throughout time flowers were used as oracles, traditions, omens, and for healing purposes. Beginning in the Orient, and later in Victorian England each type of flower was associated with a particular meaning.

A flower is the reproductive organ of a plant and has one of the highest forms of vibrational energy. Scientific study has proven that plants can and do react to human emotions and music.

Flowers traditionally symbolize beauty, life, transition, growth, happiness, friendship, peace, and awakening spirituality. Reflecting on flowers may help you solve physical, emotional, emotional or spiritual problems.

DISCOVERY 1

Selecting Your Flower Symbols

Look at the chart and pick out three of your favorite flowers. Fill in your personal symbol chart. The flowers you selected may represent your personality traits or something you may desire or need in your life.

DISCOVERY 2

Using Your Flower Symbols

1. Send a message to someone you care about. Give them a gift of the type of flower that portrays that flower's meaning as your message.
2. Choose a type flower as your personal symbol and keep them around your home.
3. Think of something you need or want. Look at the flower meanings and select the appropriate flower that will help you manifest your goal. Place the flower in a vase before you, close your eyes and meditate. As you meditate, listen, and remember any messages that you receive.

Visualization
Your Secret Healing Garden

Find a comfortable place and close your eyes. Relax an breathe deeply clearing your mind of all thoughts. As you get deeper relaxed imagine yourself in a garden. The sky is the most beautiful blue overhead with soft wispy clouds. The sun is shining and the temperature is just right for you. You can see beautiful flowers all around you. Look at the colors. Smell the wonderful aromas. You know that this is your healing garden and you can feel the energy of the flowers surround and embrace you. Making you feel whole and healthy in this time, in this place, right now. Feel how relaxed and calm your mind is. Feel your emotions as they shift to positive ones as you smell the beautiful aroma of the flowers. You feel happy, safe and secure in this garden. Smell the aroma of the flowers that have come to help heal your body...your mind...your spirit. Making you whole...healthy and happy in this wonderful, magical secret healing garden. You feel, know and trust you are healing. Feeling healthy in mind, body and spirit. Stay in the garden as long as you want and when you are ready, open your eyes.

~ FLOWERS ~

FLOWER CHART

Flower	Meaning	Flower	Meaning
Agave	Courage, Self-Awareness	Honeysuckle	Emotional Protection
Aster	Understanding, Inner Peace	Hyacinth	Ascension, Soul Repair
Azalea	Inner Knowing, Healing	Hydrangea	Honesty, Personal Truth
Bird of Paradise	Intent, Purpose	Impatiens	Energy, Healing
Bleeding Heart	Hope, Strength, Being Now	Iris	Grace, Hope, Trust
Bromeliad	Compassion, Will to Live	Jacaranda	Karmic Healing
Bouganvillea	Joyful Old Age, Acceptance	Jasmine	Harmony, Peace, Union
Buttercup	Inner Change, Purification	Lantana	Emotional Rescue
California Poppy	Stabilizing, Aids Despair	Lilac	Clarity, Relaxation
Camellia	Good Health, Compassion, Mental Strength, Stabilizes New Relationships & Marriages, Enlightenment	Lily, Calla Canna Spider Tiger Water	Purification, Enlightenment Vitality, Stability Artistic Creation Fertility, Sexuality Spiritual Wisdom
Carnation, Pink Red White	Motherhood Love, Admiration Purest Love	Lobelia	Support, Aids Change
Christmas Cactus	Balance, Emotional Rebirth	Lotus	Light, Immortality
Chrysanthemum	Happiness, Wealth	Magnolia	Spiritual Awareness
Clematis	Spiritual Purpose	Moonflower	Conscious Awareness
Clover	Spirituality, Clears Emotion	Morning Glory	Telepathy
Cosmos	Honor, Forgiveness	Narcissus	Cooperation, Harmony
Crape Myrtle	Responsibility	Nasturtium	Focus, Mind Balance
Dahlia	Spiritual Growth, Healing	Orange Blossom	Trust, Self-Love
Daisy	Innocence, Freedom	Passion Flower	Oneness, Protection
Dandelion	Heals the Past	Peony	Good Fortune, Love
FrangiPani	Receptivity, Courage	Poinsettia	Courage, Determination
Gardenia	Soul Healing	Roses, Red	Divine Light, Joy, Love
Gazania	Happiness, Self-Confidence	Rose, Gold Pink Yellow White	Spiritual Perfection Unconditional Love Friendship Purity
Geranium	Energy, Spirituality	Stephanotis	Calmness, Balance
Gladiolus	Healing, Will, Innocence	Sunflower	Abundance, Success
Gloxinia	Universal Love, Love	Sweet Pea	Life Path Acceptance
Grapefruit Blossom	Clarity, Stress Release	Tulip	Perfect Love
Heather	Spiritual Strength, Comfort	Violet	Spiritual Truth, Virtue
Hibiscus	Attachment Release, Peace	Yarrow	Emotional Healing
Hollyhock	Acceptance	Wisteria	Self-Healing

Gods & Goddesses

In every culture, humankind has many legends and myths about Gods and Goddesses. Even today some people revere, worship and celebrate them. Gods and Goddesses provided answers to the things in nature and life that defied explanation. In some cases, the ancient Gods and Goddesses were used as symbolic images that related to the parts of life that the individual could not control.

Today we can use Gods and Goddesses as archetypal symbols, or symbolic images, to help ease the path through life by looking at things in a new way. If you select a God or Goddess, look into their legend to define their strength, weakness and actions. You may find similarities or situations that relate to your own present life. Seeing how they handled their situation may bring you insight into how you can handle your current situation. Think about and write down the similarities and the differences between you and your God and Goddess symbols to find out your answers.

DISCOVERY 1

Selecting & Using Your God and Goddess Symbols

Look at the chart and pick out your favorite God and Goddess. Fill in your personal symbol chart. One way to use these charts is to meditate on your selected God or Goddess name before you go to sleep and see if you wake up with a message or clarity of your situation.

~ GODS & GODDESSES ~

ANCIENT GOD CHART

Name	Origin	Description	Name	Origin	Description
Aani	Egypt	Dog Headed Ape	Krishna	Hindu	Avatar of Vishnu
Abu (Aku)	Babylon	Sky, Sun	Ler	Celtic	Sea
Adad (Adda)	Babylon	Wind, Storm	Loki (Lok)	Norse	Discord, Mischief
Aegir	Norse	Sea	Lugh	Celtic	Sun, Light
Aesculapius	Greek/Roman	Medicine	Mars	Roman	War
Agni	Hindu	Fire	Ment	Egypt	Falcon Headed
Akal	Hindu	Immortal	Min	Egypt	Procreation
Amen (Amon)	Egypt	King, Sun	Momus	Greek	Ridicule
Amor	Roman	Love	Mors	Roman	Death
Anat	Assyrian	Sky	Nabu (Nebu)	Babylon	Wisdom
Apollo	Greek	Sun, Prophecy	Neptune	Roman	Sea
Apsu (Assur)	Babylon	Chaos	Nereus	Greek	Sea
Ares	Greek	War	Odin	Norse	Chief, Wisdom
Asun	Assyrian	War	Orcus	Roman	Dead
Babbar	Babylon	Sun	Osiris	Egypt	Underworld
Bacchus	Roman	Wine	Pan	Greek	Flocks, Forest
Balder	Norse	Light	Pluto	Greek	Underworld
Bel	Babylon	Chief	Plutus	Greek	Wealth
Bes	Egypt	Pleasure	Poseidon	Greek	Sea
Bragi	Norse	Poetry	Ptah	Egypt	Memphis
Civa (Siva)	Hindu	Supreme	Ra	Egypt	Sun
Comus	Greek/Roman	Mirth, Revelry	Rama	Hindu	Vishnu
Cronus	Greek	Titan	Set (Seth)	Egypt	Evil
Cupid	Roman	Love	Shamash	Babylon	Sun
Dagan	Babylon	Earth	Sin (Enzu)	Babylon	Moon
Dagda	Celtic	Chief	Siris	Babylon	Alcohol
Deva (Dewa)	Hindu	Divine Being	Sobk	Egypt	Crocodile Headed
Dis	Greek/Roman	Underworld	Sol	Roman	Sun
Dylan	Welsh	Chief	Su	Egypt	Solar
Ea (Hea, Enki)	Babylon	Chief	Tem	Egypt	Sun
Er	Norse	War	Thor	Norse	Thunder
Eros	Greek	Love	Thoth	Egypt	Wisdom, Magic
Etana	Babylon	Eagle Rider	Triton	Greek	Sea
Eurus	Greek	Southeast Wind	Ty	Norse	Sky, War
Frey	Norse	Fertility	Utug	Babylon	Sun
Hades	Greek	Underworld	Van	Norse	Sea
Helios	Greek	Sun	Vayu	Hindu	Wind
Hermes	Greek	Herald	Vishnu	Hindu	Supreme
Horus	Egypt	Hawk Headed	Vulcan	Roman	Fire
Inti	Incan	Sun	Yama	Hindu	Judge of the Dead
Ira	Babylon	War	Zeus	Greek	God Head
Jove	Roman	Chief God	Zio	Norse	Sky

ANCIENT GODDESS CHART

Name	Origin	Description	Name	Origin	Description
Ai (Aya)	Babylon	Shamash Consort	Isis	Egypt	Fertility
Ana (Anu)	Celtic	Mother, Queen	Ishtar	Babylon	Love, Chief
Anta (Apet)	Egypt	Maternity	Juno	Roman	Queen
Aphrodite	Greek	Love	Kali	Hindu	Change, Evil
Ara	Greek	Destruction	Lachesis	Greek	Thread Length
Artemis	Greek	Moon, Nature	Luna	Roman	Moon
Astarte	Phoenician	Love, Fertility	Maat (Mut)	Egypt	Truth, Justice
Ate	Greek	Discord, Mischief	Matris	Babylon	Mothers
Athena	Greek	Wisdom	Minerva	Celtic	Wisdom
Atropos	Greek	Thread Cutter	Moira	Egypt	Fate
Aurora	Roman	Dawn	Morn	Greek	Fate
Bast	Egypt	Cat-Headed	Nanai	Babylon	Anu's Daughter
Buto	Egypt	Serpent	Nemesis	Greek	Revenge
Ceres	Roman	Earth	Nike	Greek	Victory
Chloris	Greek	Flowers	Nina	Babylon	Watery Deep
Clotho	Greek	Thread Spinner	Nona	Roman	Fate
Cybele	Greek	Nature	Nox	Roman	Night
Demeter	Greek	Agriculture	Nut	Egypt	Heaven
Devi	Hindu	Divinity	Ops	Roman	Harvest
Diana	Roman	Moon, Hunt	Pele	Hawaii	Fire, Volcanoes
Don	Brythonic	God's Ancestor	Ran	Norse	Sea
Eir	Greek/Norse	Healing	Rhea	Greek	Mother of Gods
Eos	Greek	Dawn	Salus	Roman	Prosperity
Epona	Roman	Horses	Sati	Egypt	Queen
Erda	Norse	Earth	Selena	Greek	Moon
Eris	Greek	Discord	Spes	Roman	Hope
Erua	Babylon	Mother	Sri (Lakshmi)	Hindu	Beauty, Luck
Flora	Roman	Flowers	Terra	Roman	Earth
Freya	Norse	Love, Beauty	Uma	Hindu	Splendor
Ge (Gaia)	Greek	Earth Mother	Urd	Norse	Destiny
Hathor	Egypt	Love, Mirth	Usas	Hindu	Dawn
Hecate	Greek	Moon, Magic	Vac	Hindu	Speech
Hel	Norse	Underworld	Venus	Roman	Love
Hera	Greek	Queen	Vesta	Roman	Hearth
Iris	Roman	Rainbow	Vor	Norse	Betrothal

DISCOVERY 2

Selecting Your Goddess Sub Symbols

The Goddess has always had her own set of sub-symbols throughout time. The symbols in the following chart are base on archaeological findings and interpretations of their meanings to the Goddess. You can use these sub-symbols to remind you of what you want to accomplish. Making or finding a sub-symbol and keeping it with you will remind you of your purpose. Select one of these Goddess sub-symbols and place it in your fill in your chart.

GODDESS SYMBOLS

Goddess Symbol	Meaning
Amphibian	Regeneration
Bear	Birth Giver
Bee	Regeneration
Bird	Giver of All
Bull	Source of Life
Butterfly	Regeneration
Circle	Divine Energy Center
Crescent	Energy
Doe	Mother
White Dog	Death
Dove	Soul
Duck	Luck, Wealth
Egg	Regeneration
The Letter - M	Life Giver
Owl	Death Messenger
Ram	Magic
Snake	Life Source
Sow	Earth Mother

DISCOVERY 3

Selecting Your Zodiac Goddess Symbols

There are Goddess signs of the Zodiac. To select yours find your Zodiac sign or birth date in the chart below and fill in your Zodiac Goddess name on your fill-in chart.

ZODIAC GODDESS SYMBOLS

Zodiac Sign	Birth Dates	Goddess
Aries	3/21-4/20	Minerva
Taurus	4/21-5/21	Isis
Gemini	5/22-6/21	Kali
Cancer	6/22-7/23	Selene
Leo	7/24-8/23	Juno
Virgo	8/24-9/23	Diana
Libra	9/24-10/23	Ishtar
Scorpio	10/24-11/22	Pele
Sagittarius	11/23-12/22	Artemis
Capricorn	12/23-1/20	Vesta
Aquarius	1/21-2/18	Iris
Pisces	2/19-3/20	Aphrodite

Native American Animal Spirit Guides

Belief in Animal Spirits comes from the Native American's basic belief system that all natural objects on earth and in the universe have souls and spirits. This is called Animism. Sometimes a Native American Animal Spirit encompasses not just the individual essence of the animal you see, but of all the animal essences of its species since the species began.

According to the Native American tradition Spirit Animals can help human beings by guiding, teaching and perhaps even providing protection for them. Sometimes a 'Spirit' Animal can give a person power using one or more of the Animal Spirit's traits. In the Native American tradition each Animal Spirit has a specific meaning, significance and their own characteristics.

There are several ways in which you can communicate with an Animal Spirit or they can communicate with you. It can be done through meditation or a Vision Quest, which can be an attempt to achieve a vision of a future guardian spirit through fasting or other methods. You can see an Animal Spirit in your dreams or you may see the Animal Spirit in real life as it crosses your path. All these ways may have a meaning or a message for you from the Animal Spirit.

In this book there are three ways to find and work with your Native American Animal Spirits. You'll be able to find your own Animal Spirit Guide, learn what an Animal Spirit is trying to communicate to you, or how you can communicate with them, and discover the meaning of what a Native American Animal Spirit means when they appear in a dream.

DISCOVERY 1

Finding Your Native American Animal Spirit Guide

Sometimes you may be drawn to a particular animal for no apparent reason. Sometimes an animal will find you and will cross your path again and again. This may be your Animal Spirit Guide. Each Spirit Animal has its own meaning and different Animal Spirit Guides may help guide, teach or protect you at different times in your life. To find your own Native American Animal Spirit Guide think about an a particular animal you like or always seems to be drawn to you. You can also look at the Native American Animal Spirit names in the charts in this chapter. The meanings are unimportant, just feel which animal's name is right for you.

Visualization
Meeting Your Animal Guide

Now sit in a quiet spot and state your intention that you would like to meet your Native American Animal Spirit Guide. Close your eyes. Breathe deeply and slowly as you relax your mind. Imagine you are alone in a beautiful spot surrounded by Nature. You feel safe, calm and relaxed, without a care or worry. Be still as you watch your Native American Spirit Guide come to you. Feeling loved, protected, you are filled with gratitude and respect. Listen as your Animal Spirit Guide talks, whether silently or with words, you hear and understand all they are saying. When you are done thank your Native American Animal Spirit Guide and open your eyes.

If you discovered your animal spirit guide place the information in your fill-in chart. If you didn't, try this visualization again or perhaps you will meet your guide in a dream or the very next time you go outside. Be open and eventually your animal spirit guide will come forth.

DISCOVERY 2

Communicating with Native American Spirit Animals

The following charts provides a key word as to the meaning of the Animal Spirit's messages whom you may run across or see in real life. The charts can also be used to discern the meaning of why you suddenly see or find yourself drawn to or have an affinity for a specific animal.

Another way to foster communication is to meditate on a specific Animal Spirit to see if it will communicate with you and help provide answers to your questions. You may even want to ask the animal for help or to foster you with a particular strength of the animal to help you get through a situation. When you meditate you can ask the animal, with respect, to help you.

Another way to use this charts is ask to dream about the Native American Animal Spirit before you go to sleep. Keep a pen or pencil and paper by your bedside. When you wake up, try to remember if there was a message or if you have more clarity about your situation. Write down any words or impressions about your dream.

NATIVE AMERICAN ANIMAL SPIRIT COMMUNICATION

Animal - Meaning	Animal - Meaning
Antelope - Action	Cow - Docile
Armadillo - Defense	Coyote - Cunning
Badger - Aggressive	Cricket - Disharmony
Bat - Macabre	Crow - Portent
Bear - Strength	Deer - Lowliness
Beaver - Resourceful	Dog - Loyalty
Beetle - Hidden Knowledge	Donkey - Helpful
Bighorn Sheep - Conqueror	Dolphin - Universal Mind
Bull - Sexual Energy	Duck (Wild) - Adventure
Buffalo - Abundance	Eagle - Spirit Messenger
Butterfly - Friendly	Elk - Brave
Canary - Joy	Falcon - Soul Healing
Cardinal - Beauty	Flamingo - Grace
Cat - Independent	Fly - Parasitic
Chickadee - Optimism	Fox - Wily
Chicken - Foolish	Frog - Sorcery
Chameleon - Adaptable	Goose (Snow) - Fidelity Goose (Domestic) - Quarrelsome
Cockroach - Survival	Hawk - Opportunity
Heron - Spiritual	Pig - Intelligence
Horse - Freedom	Porcupine - Protection
Hummingbird - Joy	Possum - Avoidance
Lark - Weather	Quail - Family
Lizard - Old Wisdom	Rabbit - Gentle
Lynx - Psychic	Raccoon - Enterprising
Magpie - Knowledge	Rat - Survival
Meadowlark - Protection	Raven - Bringer of Light
Mole - Trust	Sea Gull - Freedom
Moose - Longevity	Skunk - Defense
Mouse - Busy	Snake - Raw Energy
Mountain Lion - Leader	Spider - Fate
Mule - Stubborn	Squirrel - Resourceful
Owl - Diviner	Turkey - Forgetful
Otter - Playful	Turtle - Self Reliance
Pheasant - Guise	Whale - Consciousness
Pigeon (In Air) - Mission Pigeon (On Ground) - Inertia	Wolf - Organize
Pelican - Saver	Woodpecker - Resourceful

Native American Animal Dream Spirit

If an animal appears in your dream it has a meaning or they are trying to tell you something. Look at the chart and pick out the animal that was in your dream and see how the meaning applies to you. The meaning is a base to start interpreting the Animal Spirits in your own dreams. Since your perception and dreams are unique for you, please remember that this is just the start of your discovery and that your interpretation is as unique as you are.

NATIVE AMERICAN ANIMAL DREAM SPIRIT

Animal	Meaning	Animal	Meaning
Badger	Someone is pushing you. You are not fighting back	Hare	Be aware of beauty around you
Bear	Use your Power and help	Horse	Take risks. Personal freedom suppressed
Beaver	Get busy & complete project	Mouse	Tendency to Talk. No insight.
Buffalo	Develop leadership qualities	Owl	Tremendous undeveloped psychic potential
Coyote	Put more fun in your life	Raccoon	Get Organized. Have more fun.
Crow	Get help to discover betrayal	Ram	Seek spiritual not material pleasures
Deer	Need for beauty and gentleness	Sea Gull	Get out of old pattern
Dolphin/ Whale	Community concerns	Skunk	Need for protection and defense
Eagle / Hawk	Growth and important lessons	Snake	Use your wisdom and intelligence
Elk / Moose	Need to balance male/female energy. Contact opposite sex	Songbird	Missing artistic beauty in your life
Frog	Expand your Spirituality	Turtle	Slow down and be patient
Fox	Be More Cunning	Wolf	Neglecting family needs

Numbers

There are more to numbers than just meaning the quantity or measurement of something. In fact, Plato thought the study of number symbols to be the highest level of knowledge. Pythagoras, another ancient Greek philosopher, thought numbers had souls and magical powers.

As far as primary numbers, in the Eastern World the first 12 numbers symbolize the Spirit and its journey or where you are at on your Spirit Path. In the Western World the first 10 numbers are the primary numbers and symbolize this. Each number is has associated traits and characteristics.

There are number symbols all around us. When some of these numbers pop up you may feel that something about them is significant. Even when you meditate, dream or unexpectedly come across or have an experience with an exact number, this number is probably of great significance to you. Different from numerology, which we will get into in the next chapter, Number symbols can be used as a favorite number, a lucky number or even to discern messages meant for you.

DISCOVERY 1

Finding Your Favorite and Lucky Numbers

Many of you may already have or know your favorite number and your lucky number. If you know them — write them into your fill-in chart. Then look at the chart to see the characteristics and traits of your numbers. If you don't know your favorite and lucky numbers, your unconscious mind is a powerful tool you can use to help you decide which numbers are yours. To discover your favorite and lucky number you can either wait and see what numbers come up in your life or try this exercises.

Visualization
The Dark Number Pool

Find a quiet space and concentrate on your breath and breathing. Now imagine you are in a dark cave sitting before a dark underground pool of water. You look up and through a small hole in the cave's ceiling you see a Light. The Light shines down into the pool and as you look at the water's surface a number appears outlined in the Light. You know that this number is your favorite number. Watch as this number disappears and the pool becomes dark again. Another number is now coming into view. You know this is your lucky number or a number that has a significant meaning in your life. You will remember these numbers. Now watch as this number fades away. Open your eyes and write these numbers into your fill-in chart.

DISCOVERY 2

Using the Numbers Chart

You can use the following number charts in several ways. One way is to look up your favorite and lucky numbers on the chart to learn the meaning of the numbers and what their traits and characteristics are. If your specific number does not appear on the chart, then combine the words that seem right to you from the individual digits in the chart that make up your number.

The second way to use the charts is to discover the meaning of a particular number that comes into your life and feels significant to you in a particular moment, or if you dream about a number. Then you can look up the meaning of that number in the charts to help clarify understanding of the number's message and significance to you. At the very least it can help give you a direction of where to start to get further information about that number.

The third way is to use the following 'The Dark Number Pool 2' visualization and chart as a tool to get answers to questions you may have.

Visualization
The Dark Number Pool 2

Find a quiet space and state your intention. (e.g., "I want to know the number that can help me answer my question (*state the question*)." Now concentrate on your breath and breathing. Imagine you are in a dark cave sitting before a dark underground pool of water. You look up and through a small hole in the cave's ceiling you see a Light. The Light shines down into the pool and as you look at the water's surface a number or several numbers appears outlined in the Light. You know the numbers are significant. You will remember these numbers. Now watch as this numbers disappear. Keep still and wait to see if any other numbers appear in the pool. If any appear you will remember these too. When you are done watch as the numbers fade away. Look up at the Light at the top of the cave and give thanks to what has happened here today. Now open your eyes and find your numbers in the charts.

~ NUMBERS ~

PRIMARY SPIRIT NUMBERS

Number	Meaning	Color	Astro Sign	Planet	Symbol
1	Leader, Individual, Unity, Spiritual Essence	Red	Leo, Aquarius	Sun, Mercury	Circle, Rose
2	Partnership, Duality, Association, Reflection	Orange	Cancer	Moon	Yin/Yang
3	Self-Expression, Mysticism, Good Fortune	Yellow	Sagittarius, Pisces	Moon, Jupiter	Triangle
4	Stability, Organization, Practical, Balance	Green	Leo, Aquarius	Uranus, Mercury	Cross, Pyramid
5	Marriage, Human Life, Love, Freedom	Blue	Gemini, Virgo	Venus	Pentagram
6	Perfection, Accomplishment Responsibility	Purple	Taurus, Libra	Venus	Star of David
7	Wisdom, Sacred, Healing	Black	Cancer	Neptune, Venus	Rainbow
8	Reality, Abundance Achievement, Totality	Grey	Capricorn	Saturn	Infinity
9	Self-Awareness, Compassion, Truth	White	Aries, Scorpio	Moon, Mars	Alpha and Omega
10	Perfection, Completion, Holy				
11	Transition, Inspiration, Spiritual Messenger				
12	Heaven, Divine Spirit, Cosmic Order				

SIGNIFICANT SPIRIT NUMBERS

Number	Meaning	Number	Meaning
13	Renewal	33	Master Teacher
14	Justice	36	Cosmic Relationship
15	Completeness	40	Intuition
16	Nature	50	Spiritual Quest
20	Wholeness	60	Longevity
21	Divine Wisdom	100	Paradise

Numerology

Numerology is based in science with a background of ancient past wisdoms and moral philosophies. Numerology appears in Egypt and Babylon, and was used in ancient China, Rome, Japan and Greece. It is said that Pythagoras was credited as the Founding Father in the field of modern day numerology.

The theory behind numerology is that each number resonates to a particular vibration. It also encompasses the study of the numerical value of letters in names and words. By using a date or name numerology can tell you many things about the traits and personality of an individual person, business, world or even universal events. Numerologists believe that everything happens because of numbers and that numbers have both a positive and negative meaning. This chapter gives you only the simple basics. If you want an in-depth view research more on your own.

DISCOVERY 1

Finding Your Life Cycle Number

Your Life Cycle, also known as Life Path, number consists of your Birth Date. Use your exact birth date found on your birth certificate. If you were adopted and do not know your actual birth date then use the date you were legally adopted. After calculating your Life Cycle Number you can reference the NUMEROLOGY chart to find out some basic things about you or others you choose to do this for.

EXAMPLE: If your date of birth is December 25, 1971 you would add up the numbers like this:

Month of Birth:	12
Day of Birth:	25
Year of Birth:	1971
Total:	2008

Reduce the Total to a single digit like this:

$2 + 0 + 0 + 8 = 10$ Reduce the 2 digits one step further: $1 + 0 = 1$ Life Cycle Number

In this case **1** is the Life Cycle Number.

~ NUMEROLOGY ~

Now figure out your Life Cycle Below and place it in the fill-in chart in the back of the book.

Month of Birth: (1-12)

Day of Birth: (1-31)

Year of Birth   +_____ (four digits)

Total and Reduce: _____ = ____ + ____ + ____ + ____ = _____

Reduce One Step Further: = ____ + ____ = _____ This is Your Life Cycle Number.

This is the Classical conversion chart used to give letters their numeric equivalents.

LETTER-TO-NUMBER CONVERSION CHART

1	2	3	4	5	6	7	8	9
A	B	C	D	E	F	G	H	I
J	K	L	M	N	O	P	Q	R
S	T	U	V	W	X	Y	Z	

DISCOVERY 2

Finding Your Life Balance Number

Although a minor number in Numerology, your balance number becomes important if you are going through emotional upheaval, turmoil or trauma. Your Balance number can give you the guidance you need on how best to deal with the situation. To find your balance number you will be using the initials of your first, middle and last name, usually found on your birth certificate or if adopted the name you were born with, if known. If you have changed your name, you can use that but remember the original name you were born with still will give the highest vibration. Once you have calculated your Life Balance Number place it in your fill-in chart.

EXAMPLE: If your name on your birth certificate was Lisa Marie Smith you would use the initial L - M - S. Now go to the LETTER-TO-NUMBER CONVERSION CHART, find the letter's numerical values and add them together to get your balance number.

    L + M + S

    3 + 4 + 1 = 8

Now figure out your Life Cycle Below and place it in the fill-in chart in the back of the book.

INITIAL: First _____ Middle _____ Last _____

NUMBER: _____ + _____ + _____ = _____ Balance Number

Your balance can help you in an emotional situation. Just go to the NUMEROLOGY Chart, look for your number. Find your number and go to the column called QUALITIES and select the quality that might help you get back to balance or help you in your current emotional situation.

DISCOVERY 3

Finding Your Life Destiny Number

Your Life Destiny Number, also known as your Expression Number, is your entire self. It represents your identity, disposition, personality, character, temperament, even your nature. It describes the way you express yourself in the world.

To find your destiny number you should always use the full name as found on the birth certificate or if adopted, the name you were born with, if known. Again if you have changed your name or use the name you are most known by remember the original name you were born with still has the highest vibration. Once you calculate your Life Destiny Number to find information about you look at the NUMEROLOGY chart and place your Life Destiny your fill-in chart.

EXAMPLE: If your name on your birth certificate was Lisa Smith go to the LETTER-TO-NUMBER CONVERSION CHART, find the letter's numerical values and add them together.

L +I +S +A +M +A +R +I +E +S +M +I +T +H

3 +9 +1 +1 +4 +1 +9 + 9 +5 + 1 +4 +9 +2 +8 = 66 TOTAL

TOTAL REDUCED 66 = 6+6 = 12

12 = 1+2 = 3 The Life Destiny Number is 3.

Now figure out your Life Destiny Number:

Name: First _____ Middle _____ Last Name _____

Number: = _____ TOTAL

TOTAL REDUCED:

NUMEROLOGY

#	Symbol	Planet	Cycles	Qualities	Love	Vocation	Money
1	Circle, Rose	Sun	Jan 1 - Feb 9 New Beginnings	Pioneer, Innovators, Vision, Outgoing, Benevolence, Protector, Creative, Unchanging	Best: 2, 6 Others: 3, 4, 5, 7	Artist Business Scientist Educator Engineer Producer Administrator	Risk Takers
2	Yin/Yang	Moon	Feb 10 - Mar 21 Seeking Knowledge	Cooperative, Gentle, Sensitive, Helpful, Imaginative, Diplomatic, Devoted, Ever-Changing	Best: 2, 4, 6 Others: 1, 8, 3, 5	Actor Musician Psychologist Teacher Research Nurse Accountant	Secure Investor
3	Triangle	Jupiter	Mar 22 - Apr 30 Self Expression	Intellectual, Witty, Popular, Gregarious, Talented, Affectionate, Friendly, Community	Best: 1, 3, 5, 8 Others: 2, 4, 6, 7, 9	Writer Entertainer Photographer Publishing Advertising Engineer Public Relations	Easy Come, Easy Go
4	Cross, Pyramid	Saturn	May 1 - Jun 10 Making Decisions	Justice, Stubborn, Responsible, Genius, Dependable, Sacrifice, Individualist, Tolerant,	Best: 4, 7, 9 Others: 2, 6, 1, 8	Engineer Chemist Contractor Judge Lawyer Mathematician Craftsman Pharmacist	Prudent, Thrifty
5	Pentagram	Mercury	Jun 11 - Jul 21 New Pleasures	Intelligent, Bold, Adaptable, Sensuous, Impulsive, Versatile, Dynamic, Decisive, Enthusiastic	Best: 5, 3, 6 Others: 7, 8	Writer Journalist Artist, Criminal Law Aviator Stock Broker Public Relations Any Field	Generous, Casual
6	Star of David	Venus	Jul 22 - Aug 31 Increased Awareness	Harmonious, Beautiful, Balanced, Compassionate, Team Player, Courteous, Prideful, Romantic	Best: 6, 2 Others: 3, 5, 4	Teacher Doctor Social Worker Nurse Bookkeeper Accountant	Security

NUMEROLOGY *(cont.)*

#	Symbol	Planet	Cycles	Qualities	Love	Vocation	Money
7	Rainbow	Uranus	Sep 1 - Oct 10 Solitude and Meditation	Intelligent, Intuitive, Individualist, Mysterious, Philosopher, Spiritual, Receptive	Best: 9, 4, 7 Others: 3, 5, 1, 8	Scientist Educator Artist Religion Agent Writer Navigator	Economy
8	Infinity	Mars	Oct 11 - Nov 20 Overcoming Obstacles	Strength, Patient, Successful, Determined, Powerful, Loyal, Self-Disciplined, Ambitious	Best: 2, 7, 4, 9 Others: 3, 5, 6, 2	Executive Planner Business, Authority Figure in Any Field	Well To Do, Flair
9	Alpha & Omega	Neptune	Nov 21 - Dec 31 Service to Mankind	Loves Fellow Man, Noble, Philosopher, Leader, Mystical, Inspirationalist	Best: 4, 7, 9 Others: 3, 6, 8	Doctor Social Worker Lecturer Hypnotist Law Teacher, Advertising Finance Religious Leader	Generous, Basic

Oriental Horoscope

The Oriental Horoscope has existed for thousands of years and about 2000 years ago the actual signs were named. Since 1940 modern Communist China has discouraged its use. However there are many practitioners in Thailand, Vietnam, Korea, Hong Kong and other parts of Southeast Asia.

As in the Western Astrology system, the Oriental Horoscope also has 12 signs. Here they are:

ORIENTAL ASTROLOGY SYMBOLS

RAT	DRAGON	MONKEY
OX / BUFFALO	SNAKE	ROOSTER
TIGER	HORSE	DOG
RABBIT	GOAT/SHEEP	PIG/BOAR

Whereas, Western Astrology is based on a solar calendar, the Oriental Horoscope is based on the Lunar Calendar. Another difference is that in the West our New Year begins on January 1. However, the Oriental New Year can begin anywhere between January 21 to February 18 depending upon the date when the new moon is in Aquarius.

Many Asians use the Oriental Horoscope for funerals, marriages, job changes, purchases, building sites and more. This chapter gives you a very small overview of Oriental Horoscopes and if you want to learn more I encourage you to research on your own. Here are some well-known people by their Oriental Horoscope sign.

Sign	Famous People
RAT	Roy Orbison, Vanesa Redgrave, Spencer Tracy, Marlon Brando
OX, BUFFALO	Charlie Chaplin, Jessica Lange, Bruce Springsteen, Princess Diana
TIGER	Beethoven, Phil Collins, Tom Cruise, Jodie Foster, Princess Anne
RABBIT	Johnny Depp, Lily Tomlin, Cary Grant, Julian Lennon, Bob Hope
DRAGON	John Lennon, Oprah Winfrey, Shirley Temple, Ringo Star, Jackie Gleason
SNAKE	Martin Luther King, Edgar Allan Poe, Frank Sinatra, Jackie Kennedy
HORSE	Jimi Hendrix, Ray Charles, Paul McCartney, Princess Margaret
GOAT, SHEEP	Mark Twain, Rita Hayworth, George Harrison, Whoopi Goldberg
MONKEY	Melanie Griffith, Bette Davis, Jimmy Stewart, Elizabeth Taylor
ROOSTER	Diane Keaton, Donny Wahlberg, Yoko Ono, Bette Midler, Tom Selleck
DOG	Jamie Lee Curtis, Sophia Loren, Madonna, Cher, Albert Einstein
PIG, BOAR	Stephen King, Ernest Hemingway, Carol Burnett, Julie Andrews

DISCOVERY 1

Finding Your Oriental Horoscope Sign

To see what your Oriental Horoscope sign is you will need to look at the following chart for the year you were born on the following chart. If you were born prior to January 21 of any given year your actual Oriental Horoscope sign will be the previous Western Calendar year.

Sign	Recent Years
RAT	1924, 1936, 1948, 1960, 1972, 1984, 1996, 2008, 2020, 2032
OX, BUFFALO	1925, 1937, 1949, 1961, 1973, 1985, 1997, 2009, 2021, 2033
TIGER	1926, 1938, 1950, 1962, 1974, 1986, 1998, 2010, 2022, 2034
RABBIT	1927, 1939, 1951, 1963, 1975, 1987, 1999, 2011, 2023, 2035
DRAGON	1928, 1940, 1952, 1964, 1976, 1988, 2000, 2012, 2024, 2036
SNAKE	1929, 1941, 1953, 1965, 1977, 1989, 2001, 2013, 2025, 2037
HORSE	1930, 1942, 1954, 1966, 1978, 1990, 2002, 2014, 2026, 2038
GOAT, SHEEP	1931, 1943, 1955, 1967, 1979, 1991, 2003, 2015, 2027, 2039
MONKEY	1932, 1944, 1956, 1968, 1980, 1992, 2004, 2016, 2028, 2040
ROOSTER	1933, 1945, 1957, 1969, 1981, 1993, 2005, 2017, 2029, 2041
DOG	1934, 1946, 1958, 1970, 1982, 1994, 2006, 2018, 2030, 2042
PIG, BOAR	1935, 1947, 1959, 1971, 1983, 1995, 2007, 2019, 2031, 2043

Now that you have found your sign, look at the chart below and fill-in your Personal chart.

ORIENTAL HOROSCOPE

Sign	Qualities	Love	Best to Avoid	Element	Planet	Yin/Yang
RAT	Active Socially, Resourceful, Versatile, Kind, Quick Witted	Dragon Monkey	Goat	Water	Mercury	Yang
OX/BUFFALO	A Little Unsociable, Diligent, Determined Dependable, Strong	Snake Rooster	Horse	Earth	Saturn	Yin
TIGER	Somewhat Sociable, Brave, Confident, Competitive	Horse, Dog	Snake	Wood	Jupiter	Yang
RABBIT	Socially Discriminating, Elegant, Kind, Quiet, Responsible	Goat Pig	Dragon	Wood	Jupiter	Yin
DRAGON	Likes to Be Recognized, Enthusiastic, Confident, Intelligent	Monkey Rat	Rabbit	Earth	Saturn	Yang
SNAKE	Moderately Friendly, Wise, Intelligent, Enigmatic	Rooster Ox	Tiger	Fire	Mars	Yin
HORSE	Growing Social Circle, Energetic, Animated, Active	Dog Tiger	Ox	Fire	Mars	Yang
GOAT/SHEEP	Socializes When They Want To, Gentle, Calm, Sympathetic	Pig Rabbit	Rat	Earth	Saturn	Yin
MONKEY	Somewhat Sociable, Sharp, Smart, Curious	Rat Dragon	Pig	Metal	Venus	Yang
ROOSTER	Somewhat Sociable, Courageous, Observant, Hardworking	Ox Snake	Dog	Metal	Venus	Yin
DOG	Close Circle of Friends, Prudent, Lovely, Honest	Tiger Horse	Rooster	Earth	Saturn	Yang
PIG/BOAR	Homebody, Diligent, Compassionate, Generous	Rabbit Goat	Monkey	Water	Mercury	Yin

Palm Reading

Palm Reading, otherwise known as the art of Palmistry, is a method of telling people about their traits and their future. This is based upon the interpretation of their hand type, main lines, mounts, markings and line traits.

Although its origins are unknown, the earliest Palmistry records are from India dating around 1500 B.C. Aristotle, Galen and Hippocrates all contributed to Palmistry. It has also been found in the ancient civilizations of China, Egypt, Greece, Persia, Tibet and Britain.

It's like the geography of your life is held in the palms of your hands. The shape of your hand, your fingers, the mounts (which are the fleshy cushions on the inside of your palm underneath your fingers), the numerous lines and the markings/configurations play their part.

The lines on your palm come in all shapes and sizes but every hand contain 6 basic lines which are known as the Major Lines: Heart, Head, Life Line, Mercury, Apollo and Saturn. There is also a Marriage Line. The specific markings, or configurations include: Bars, Breaks in the Lines, Branches, Chains, Crosses, Circles, Islands, Tassels Triangles, Squares and Stars.

The charts included here will give you very simple, general information on reading your palm which you can place in your fill in chart. Research on your own for an in-depth reading. When reading the palm the left hand deals with natural tendencies, while the right hand deals with life.

DISCOVERY 1

Reading Your Palm

Start by looking at your opened right palm, and compare your palm to the charts. Please note, left handed people usually read their left palm.

~ PALM READING ~

PALM READING

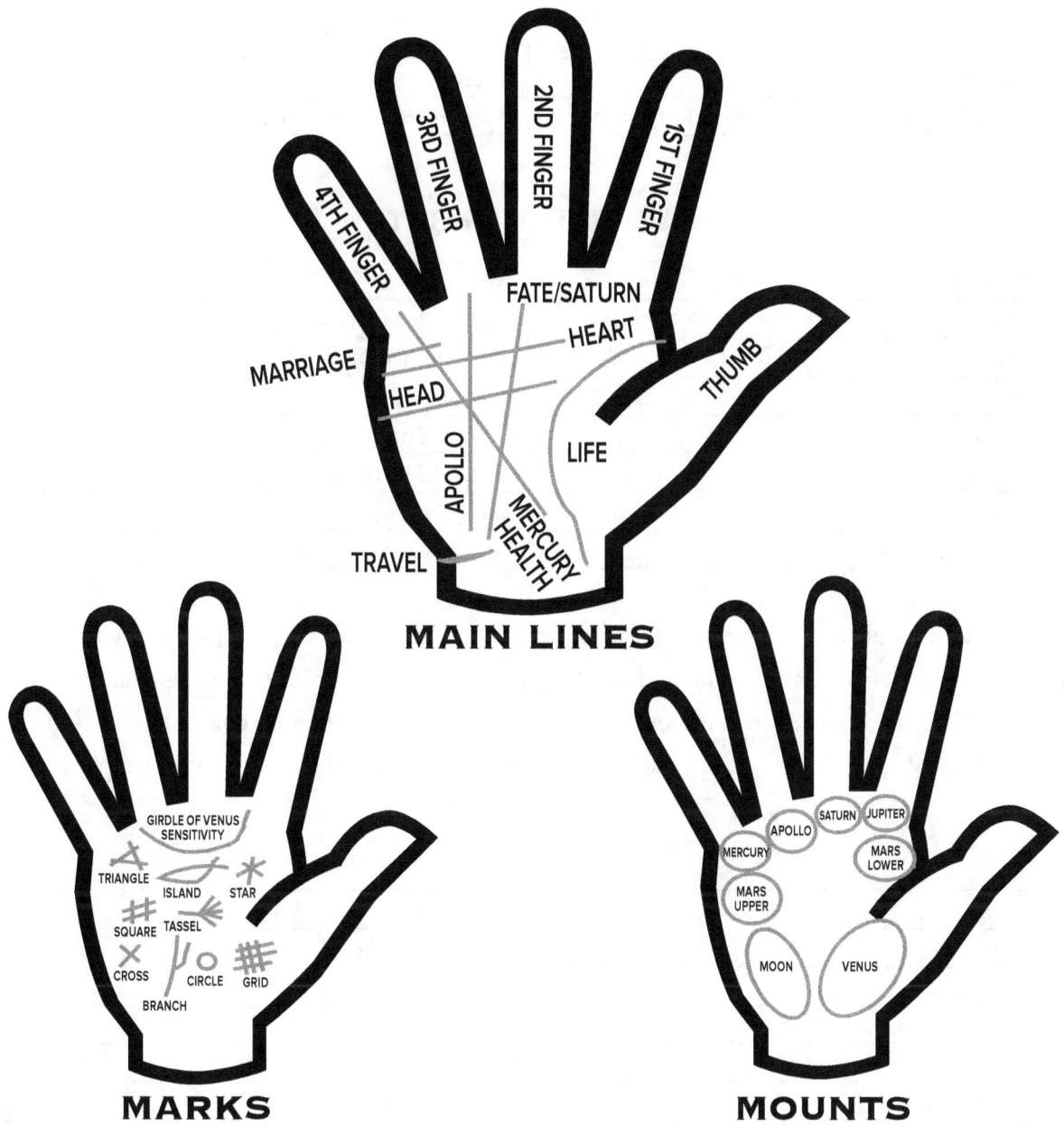

The size of someone's hand gives a clue as to how their mind works. Very small hands show immaturity and a charming personality. Large hands belong to analytical and can do delicate, intricate work. Here are some general meanings to discover what your hand shape means.

HAND SHAPES

Hand Type - Meaning	Hand Type - Meaning
Broad & Square - Traditional	Broad - Traditional
Long & Bony - Philosophical	Long & Narrow - Psychic, Reflective
Flared - Original Thinker	Mixed - Versatile
LEFT HAND - Deals with Natural Tendencies	RIGHT HAND - Deals with Life

MAIN LINE ATTRIBUTES

Main Lines	Attributes
Head	Intellect Reasoning & Career
Life	Life Pattern & Quality
Heart	Emotional Nature
Apollo	Creative Energy & Success
Mercury	Health & Business
Saturn	Fate & Destiny
Marriage	Relationships & Friends

The lines in your hands show the general trend of your personality. A broad hand usually has fewer and more clearly defined lines. If a broad hand has many lines they are sensitive. A long hand usually has many lines. In general women have more lines than men. Each line in a hand is related to the mount where it begins and ends. Your hands are not likely to be perfectly marked unless you are very simple or perfect.

LINE TRAITS

Line Traits	Attributes
Fine Lines	Subtle Perception
Deep Lines	Strong Feelings
Few Lines - Coarse Skin	Physical Energy
Few Lines - Delicate Skin	Intuitive Energy
Many Lines	Nervous Energy
Deep Main Lines	Deep Feelings
Deep Main Lines - High Mounts	Passionate
Main Lines in Breaks & Chains	Physical Strain
Accessory Wavering or Tangled Group Lines	Nervous, Over Stimulation
Pale Lines	Lack of Energy
Yellow Lines	Nervous, Inhibited
Red Lines	Strong Feelings
Pink Well Marked Lines	Healthy Mind & Body

The mounts in your hands show the keys to your character development. Mounts are the special areas of the hand that show your instinctive energy and how you use it. In some hands the mounts may flat, sunken in or may each have their own fleshy cushion. The name mounts refer to the area and not the padding. If you do have a fleshy padding and it is firm it shows physical energy. The area of the hand where your high padding is shows how you use your energy. If the padding is medium soft it is straightforward mental energy. A flat m with lots of lines is nervous energy. A high mount covered with lines show passionate, complex energy.

MOUNTS ATTRIBUTES

Mounts	Attributes
Mercury	Communication & Wit
Apollo	Creativity & Compassion
Saturn	Introspective, & Serious
Jupiter	Self Confidence & Leader
Lower Mars	Overcoming Obstacles, Self Control
Upper Mars	Determination & Courage
Venus	Physical & Sexual Energy
Moon	Intuition & Sentimental

Markings can be positive or negative blockages that appear in the normal flow of the mounts and lines of the palm. They indicate symbolize emotional healing, problem resolution, traumatic or separations. The meanings depend on where they are located on the palm. Vertical Lines usually represent positive energy.

MARKING ATTRIBUTES

Markings	Attributes
Bars	Interim Barriers
Break Ins	Weakness
Branches	Extra Strength
Circles	Amplify Body and Mind Health
Crosses	Upheaval
Grids	Obstacles
Islands	Delays, Problems
Quadrangles	Enhanced Personal Trait
Stars	Luck, Success
Squares	Strengthen Weak Areas
Tassels	Hindrances
Triangles	Luck

Phrenology

The method to determine personality traits by size and shape of the bumps on your head is known as Phrenology. It is based on the theories of a Viennese Scientist named Franz Joseph Gall in the 19th century. America quickly became so enamored with the science that employers actually advertised for workers with specific bumps on their head. Some women changed their hair to show off their best bumps on their head. Edgar Allan Poe even put phrenology concepts into his writings and it was the rage with the rich and famous. However by the 20th century, phrenology had lost any shred of its scientific authority.

The area of the head is divided into sections comprised of intellect, sympathies, survival, ambitions, energy, emotions and social instincts. Personality traits are associated with the bumps found in these areas.

DISCOVERY 1

Reading Your Head Bumps

Look at the PHRENOLOGY picture to discover where you should look for the bumps on your head. The examine the bumps on your head to see if any that you find correspond to the areas in the picture. After finding your bumps, refer to the charts to discover your personality traits. Then refer to the charts to discover your personality traits. Then fill in your personal chart with your bump information.

PHRENOLOGY

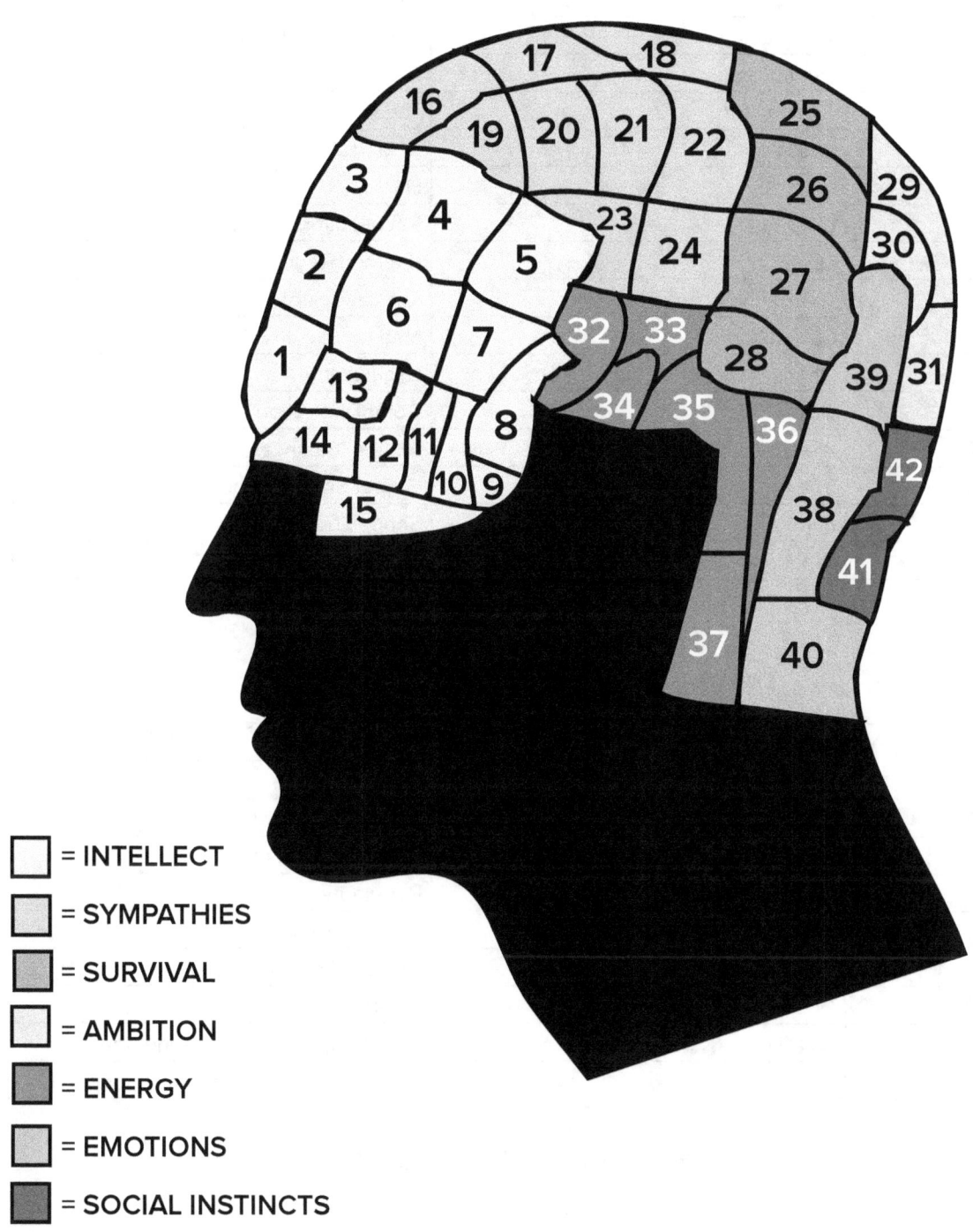

INTELLECT HEAD BUMPS

The planet Mercury is associated with the Intellect.

Area	Aspect	Bump Quality
1	Individuality	Observation, Discrimination
2	Eventuality	Memory, Current Events
3	Comparison	Judgment, Reason
4	Causality	Originality
5	Mirth	Humor
6	Locality	Recollection, Sense of Direction
7	Time	Rhythm, Regularity
8	Tune	Ear for Music
9	Calculation	Mathematical Ability
10	Order	Organization
11	Color	Color Distinction
12	Weight	Motion, Balance
13	Size	Object Size Judgment
14	Form	Shape Judgment
15	Language	Eloquence

SYMPATHIES HEAD BUMPS

The planet Jupiter is associated with Sympathies.

Area	Aspect	Bump Quality
16	Humanity	Understanding
17	Benevolence	Sympathy, Generosity
18	Veneration	Reverence, Respect
19	Agreeableness	Popularity
20	Imitation	Imitative Ability
21	Spirituality	Faith, Religious Feeling
22	Hope	Optimism
23	Ideality	Beauty Appreciation, Refinement
24	Sublimity	Love of the Best, Romantic Viewpoint

SURVIVAL HEAD BUMPS

The planet Saturn is associated with Survival.

Area	Aspect	Bump Quality
25	Firmness	Determination. Exercise of Will
26	Conscientious	Moral Fiber
27	Caution	Self Preservation
28	Secretive	Reserve, Self Restraint

AMBITIONS HEAD BUMPS

The planet Sun is associated with Ambitions.

Area	Aspect	Bump Quality
29	Self Esteem	Egotism
30	Approbativeness	Love of Praise, Desire for Approval
31	Continuity	Concentration

ENERGY HEAD BUMPS

The planet Mars is associated with Energy.

Area	Aspect	Bump Quality
32	Constructiveness	Inventiveness, Constructive Action
33	Acquisitiveness	Accumulation
34	Alimentiveness	Sustenance, Food Metabolism
35	Execution	Endurance
36	Combativeness	Courage, Aggression
37	Vitality	Zest for Life, Illness Resistance

EMOTIONS HEAD BUMPS

The planet Venus is associated with Emotions.

Area	Aspect	Bump Quality
38	Friendship	Friendship Ability, Social Affairs
39	Conjugality	Marital Status
40	Amativeness (Sexual Desire)	Sensuality, Sex Appeal

SOCIAL INSTINCTS HEAD BUMPS

The planet Moon is associated with Social Instincts.

Area	Aspect	Bump Quality
41	Inhabitiveness	Home Life
42	Parental Love	Love of Children

Planets

Planets are more than round objects in space that rotate around a Star, they have long been a source of interest and mystery. In dreams a specific Planet can symbolize an important message or a great idea. Planets even have their own energy and polarity (magnetic energy) which can be positive, negative or both. Just like the moon affects the tides and the water in our bodies with its magnetic pull, so do all the planets in our Solar System, and maybe even the Universe.

DISCOVERY 1

Finding Your Planet

As you look at the charts below you can use the planet of your astrology sign and fill in your personal chart with your planetary information.

PLANET SYMBOLS

☉	☾	☿	♀
SUN	MOON	MERCURY	VENUS

♂	♃	♄	♅
MARS	JUPITER	SATURN	URANUS

♆	♇
NEPTUNE	PLUTO

~ PLANETS ~

PLANETS 1

Planet	Sign	Musical Note	Number	Astro House	Element/Polarity	Sephirah	Rules
Sun	Leo	D	1	5th	Fire Positive	Tiphereth (Beauty)	Vitality Self Expression Leadership Creative Powers
Moon	Cancer	G Sharp A Flat	3, 9	4th	Water Negative	Jesod Foundation	Emotions Women Relationships The Night
Mercury	Gemini	E	1, 4	3rd	Air Positive/Negative	Chod (Glory)	Communication Intelligence Humor Dexterity
Venus	Taurus Libra	F Sharp G Flat	5, 6, 7	2nd 7th	Earth / Air Negative	Netzach (Victory)	Love, Beauty, Harmony, Sex, Money, Social, Partnerships
Mars	Aries	C	9	1st	Fire Positive	Geburah (Judgment)	Strength Stamina Energy Productivity
Jupiter	Sagittarius	A Sharp B Flat	3	9th 12th	Fire Positive	Chesed (Mercy)	Ethics, Truth, Luck, Legal Prosperity Opportunity
Saturn	Capricorn	A	8	10th 11th	Earth Positive	Binah (Understanding)	Patience Realism Karma Structure
Uranus	Aquarius	E	4	11th	Air Positive	-	Change, Genius Inventor Avant Garde
Neptune	Pisces	G Sharp A Flat	7	12th	Water -	-	Imagination Mysticism Secrets Unconscious
Pluto	Scorpio	C	-	8th 1st	Water -	-	Destiny Transformation Reincarnation Recycle Energy

DISCOVERY 2

Working With the Planets

If you want to work with the planets or need to stimulate the energy they rule over you can use the visualization method below. Look at the 'Rules' column in the chart and decide what you need to help you accomplish what you desire. Now look at the Planet's name associated with that rule. State this Intention before you proceed with the Visualization:

'I am asking the planet (<u>Fill in Planet Name</u>) to help me accomplish (<u>State Your Desire</u>.)"

Visualization
Planetary Energy Transfer

Find a quiet, comfortable place where you won't be distracted. Sit in a very comfortable chair with your arms and legs uncrossed. State your intention. Close your eyes and begin to quiet your mind. Just concentrate on your breath and breathing. Breathe deeply in through the nose and out with the mouth. Feel your mind quieting as your thoughts drift away. Imagine you are sitting on a cloud floating above the earth. You feel safe and all is dark around you. Suddenly you see a Light coming toward you. You know that this Light is the Planet's energy. The Light is beautiful. Feel it surround your body. You can feel the energy of the Planet come into every cell of your body — rejuvenating you, energizing you, helping you. Feel the Power. You feel, know and trust that this energy will stay with you to help you accomplish what you need and desire. Absorb all the energy you need and when you are ready — open your eyes.

PLANETS 2

Planet	Diameter (miles)	Distance From Sun (Millions of Miles)	Position Nearest the Sun	# Natural Satellites	# Days Rotation around the Sun	Metal	Gemstone
Sun	864,000					Tigers Eye Topaz Zircon	Gold Brass
Mercury	3,100	43.4M	1		88	Fire Opal Carnelian	White Alloy (No Tin/ Silver)
Venus	7,543	67.7M	2		225	Malachite Jade Coral Amber	Copper
Earth	7.926	94.6M	3	1	365 Days 24 hours		
Mars	4,200	155M	4	2	687 Days 24 Hours 37 Min	Garnet	Iron Steel
Jupiter	88,980	507M	5	16	4,332	Lapis Amethyst	Tin
Saturn	71,000	937M	6	36	10,760	Onyx Jet	Lead
Uranus	32,000	1859.7M	7	5	30,684		
Neptune	30,600	2821.7	8	2	60,188		
Pluto	1,680	4551.4	9	1	90.467		

DISCOVERY 3

Aligning with a Planet Energy

To align yourself with a planetary energy: State your specific intention and then select and carry or wear the metal or gemstone of that planet.

Playing Cards

The first mention of playing cards was in China in the Tang dynasty around the 9th century A.D. Playing Cards have been found in Ancient India, Korea, Egypt and Persia. There are 52 cards in the deck and 4 different suits. In different parts of Europe these four suits differ as shown in the chart below.

PLAYING CARDS SUITS

Country	♥	♦	♣	♠
English	Hearts	Diamond	Clubs	Spades
French	Hearts	Tiles	Clovers	Pikes
German	Hearts	Bells	Acorns	Leaves
Swiss-German	Roses	Bells	Acorns	Shields
Italian & Spanish	Cups	Coins	Clubs	Swords

Some say the four suits represent the seasons, while the thirteen cards in each suit represent the lunar cycle and the numbers on the cards equal the 365 days of the year. In medieval times it was said the four suits represent the main aspects of human nature: Hearts stand for Love, Diamonds for Money, Clubs for Knowledge and Spades for Death.

Not only were playing cards used for card games but also for education, relationship compatibility, magical rituals and divination. The ancients even had a practice of connecting birthdays to a particular card. Your birthday card number is supposed to give you insight into yourself, others and your life. There are many renditions of this practice from Love Cards, to Cards of Illumination, and beyond. If you are interested in getting a full reading or a relationship compatibility chart based on your birthday card, I encourage you to research on your own to find a credible book or practitioner.

DISCOVERY 1

Your Birthday Playing Card

The chart and method below will allow you to find your own Birthday Playing Card and it's overall life meaning. First find your birth day and then look under the month of your birth day date line. Place this into your fill-in chart. Next go the BIRTHDAY CARD MEANINGS Chart and look up your Birthday Playing Card's overall meaning and put this in your fill-in chart.

Day	Jan	Feb	Mar	Apr	May	Jun	Jul	Aug	Sep	Oct	Nov	Dec
1	K♠	J♠	9♠	7♠	5♠	3♠	A♠	Q♦	10♦	8♦	6♦	4♦
2	Q♠	10♠	8♠	6♠	4♠	2♠	K♦	J♦	9♦	7♦	5♦	3♦
3	J♠	9♠	7♠	5♠	3♠	A♠	Q♦	10♦	8♦	6♦	4♦	2♦
4	10♠	8♠	6♠	4♠	2♠	K♦	J♦	9♦	7♦	5♦	3♦	A♦
5	9♠	7♠	5♠	3♠	A♠	Q♦	10♦	8♦	6♦	4♦	2♦	K♣
6	8♠	6♠	4♠	2♠	K♦	J♦	9♦	7♦	5♦	3♦	A♦	Q♣
7	7♠	5♠	3♠	A♠	Q♦	10♦	8♦	6♦	4♦	2♦	K♣	J♣
8	6♠	4♠	2♠	K♦	J♦	9♦	7♦	5♦	3♦	A♦	Q♣	10♣
9	5♠	3♠	A♠	Q♦	10♦	8♦	6♦	4♦	2♦	K♣	J♣	9♣
10	4♠	2♠	K♦	J♦	9♦	7♦	5♦	3♦	A♦	Q♣	10♣	8♣
11	3♠	A♠	Q♦	10♦	8♦	6♦	4♦	2♦	K♣	J♣	9♣	7♣
12	2♠	K♦	J♦	9♦	7♦	5♦	3♦	A♦	Q♣	10♣	8♣	6♣
13	A♠	Q♦	10♦	8♦	6♦	4♦	2♦	K♣	J♣	9♣	7♣	5♣
14	K♦	J♦	9♦	7♦	5♦	3♦	A♦	Q♣	10♣	8♣	6♣	4♣
15	Q♦	10♦	8♦	6♦	4♦	2♦	K♣	J♣	9♣	7♣	5♣	3♣
16	J♦	9♦	7♦	5♦	3♦	A♦	Q♣	10♣	8♣	6♣	4♣	2♣
17	10♦	8♦	6♦	4♦	2♦	K♣	J♣	9♣	7♣	5♣	3♣	A♣
18	9♦	7♦	5♦	3♦	A♦	Q♣	10♣	8♣	6♣	4♣	2♣	K♥
19	8♦	6♦	4♦	2♦	K♣	J♣	9♣	7♣	5♣	3♣	A♣	Q♥
20	7♦	5♦	3♦	A♦	Q♣	10♣	8♣	6♣	4♣	2♣	K♥	J♥
21	6♦	4♦	2♦	K♣	J♣	9♣	7♣	5♣	3♣	A♣	Q♥	10♥
22	5♦	3♦	A♦	Q♣	10♣	8♣	6♣	4♣	2♣	K♥	J♥	9♥
23	4♦	2♦	K♣	J♣	9♣	7♣	5♣	3♣	A♣	Q♥	10♥	8♥
24	3♦	A♦	Q♣	10♣	8♣	6♣	4♣	2♣	K♥	J♥	9♥	7♥
25	2♦	K♣	J♣	9♣	7♣	5♣	3♣	A♣	Q♥	10♥	8♥	6♥
26	A♦	Q♣	10♣	8♣	6♣	4♣	2♣	K♥	J♥	9♥	7♥	5♥
27	K♣	J♣	9♣	7♣	5♣	3♣	A♣	Q♥	10♥	8♥	6♥	4♥
28	Q♣	10♣	8♣	6♣	4♣	2♣	K♥	J♥	9♥	7♥	5♥	3♥
29	J♣	9♣	7♣	5♣	3♣	A♣	Q♥	10♥	8♥	6♥	4♥	2♥
30	10♣		6♣	4♣	2♣	K♥	J♥	9♥	7♥	5♥	3♥	A♥
31	9♣		5♣		A♣		10♥	8♥		4♥		Joker

BIRTHDAY CARD MEANINGS

Card	♥ Meaning	♣ Meaning	♦ Meaning	♠ Meaning
Ace	Love/Money Self-Searching	Knowledge Independent	Love/Money Idealistic	Ambition/Secrets Transformation
King	Love/ Devoted Loving Father	Communication Knowledge Master	Successful/Rigid Business Authority	Wise/Powerful Master of Anything
Queen	Idealism/ Romance Loving Mother	Service/ Impatience Mother of Intuition	Higher Values Philanthropist	Self-Mastery Power/Authority
Jack	Universal Love Spiritual Power	Creative/Brilliant Mentally Inspired	Inspiration/Ideas Sharp/Clever/Sales	Leader or Thief Mental Power
10	Charming/ Promoter Group Success	Success/Indecision Knowledge/Sharing	Blessed Money Protected	Restless Mind Work Success
9	Universal Love Giver/ Humorous	Sensual/Adventure Universal Thinker	Soul Evolution The Giver	Skeptical/Artistic Universal Life
8	Responsibility Emotional Power	Mental Power Healers/Prosperity	Opportunities Intuition/Prosperity	Right Thinking Power In Work
7	Love/Truth Unconditional Love	Spirituality/Positive Material Abundance	Spiritual Values Creative/Prosperity	Work/Health Spiritual Lifestyle
6	Stable Heart/ Peace Successful	Higher Purpose Psychic Messenger	Love/Fulfillment Financial Payback	Balance/ Giver Cause and Effect
5	Variety/Change Athletic/Seeker	Adventure/Truth Intellectual Mind	Worth/Freedom Energetic/Intuitive	Loves Travel/Truth Humanitarian
4	Home/Security Successful/Healers	Love of Life Mentally Strong	Hard Work/Values Financial Protection	Stable/Hardworking Solid Relationships
3	Inquisitive/Creative Nurturing	Emotional Security Creativity/Writing	Positive Attitude Financial Creativity	Artistic/ Creativity Work = Success
2	Love/Harmony Fortunate	Communication Natural Ability	Intelligence/Power Intuitive Success	Partnership Cooperation
Joker	Youthful, Independent, Creativity, Keen Wit			

DISCOVERY 2

Playing Card Insight

Cards are also an ancient method of tapping into the subconscious mind to see the potential and possibilities of your situation. This chart and ancient 15 card spread method using standard playing cards may help you in making right decisions and find answers to your questions.

~ PLAYING CARDS ~

How to Use the 15 Card Spread:

1. Think of a Question
2. Shuffle the Card Deck Rhythmically
3. Choose a Card at anytime and proceed to lay them out as they are selected in the following order, as drawn, starting with the first card which is # 1.

Please Note: Each card's meaning is shaded by those cards around it.

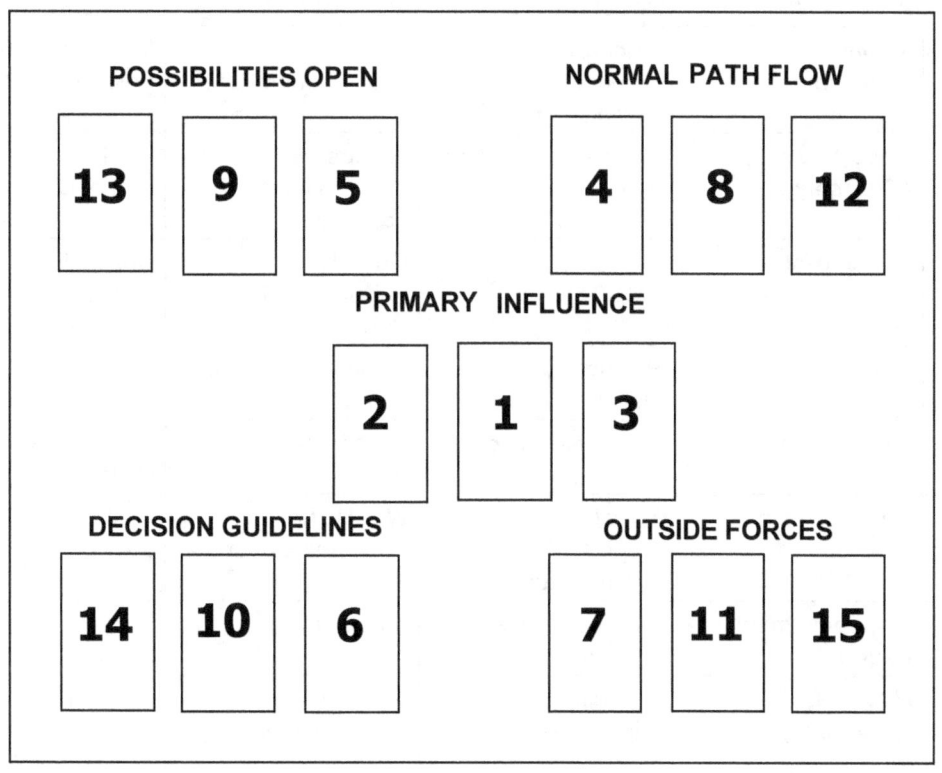

Card 1: Querent Trait or Primary Life Influence

Card 2 and 3: Querent Personality or Surrounding Situation

Card 4, 8, 12: Normal Life Path Flow

Card 13, 9, 5: Alternate Life Path; Open Possibilities

Card 14, 10, 6: Present/Future Decision Making Guidelines

Card 7, 11, 15: Outside Forces

Now find the meanings of your layout of cards in the PLAYING CARD MEANING chart.

PLAYING CARD MEANINGS

CARD	♥ MEANING	♣ MEANING	♦ MEANING	♠ MEANING
ACE	Pleasure Joy	Talent High Ambition	Money Constructive Power	Force Power
KING	Dependable Man of Good Will and Integrity	Reserved Man of Diversified Interests	Complex Man with Hidden Assets	Honest, Intelligent, Powerful Man
QUEEN	Love, Joy A Good Woman	Shrewd Woman of Social Graces	Passionate Woman with Social Prestige	Psychic Woman who Conceals Emotions
JACK	Romance Friendship	Sincere, Hard Working Young Person	Crossroads of Life	Immature Young Person
10	Good News A Messenger	Inexperienced Youth	Escape from Confinement, A Journey	Barrier, Wall End of Delusion
9	Happiness	Success, Work Satisfaction	Good Wish Fulfilled, Bad Wish Rebounded	Unpredictable Change, Catastrophe
8	Gift	Balance, Quiet Delight, Harmony	Financial/Spiritual Balance	Contentment Haven
7	Lover's Quarrel	Illusionary Success	Unresolved Financial Distress	Partial Success Division
6	Advancement Step Up	Social Life Opportunity, Good Fortune	Well Being, Economic Security	Anxiety Suspended Motion
5	Disappointment Regret	Avoid Quarrels with Friends	Clash of Wills	Separation Remorse
4	Happiness Opportunity thru Work	Strengthening Friendship	Success Business Finance	Healing Recuperation
3	Disappointment in Love	Unpleasant Social Episode	Legal Document	Sudden Resolution
2	Love Letter, Good News, Unexpected Pleasure	Social Invitation	Unexpected Communication About Money, Business	Minor Stumbling Block

Shapes, Geometric

For thousands of years, in almost every country, geometric shapes have been part of religious, scientific, mathematical and construction projects. A lot of the shapes are found in nature and are used by many different cultures as symbols with specific meanings. The shapes with curves usually represent community and connection. The shapes with lines and angles usually represent order and structure.

There are many different kinds of shapes. Organic, natural shapes, like leaves or clouds, are usually free form, curved and irregular. These shapes are comforting. Another kind of shape are abstract shapes represent an idea or concept, like a bull's eye or stick figure. Geometric shapes, are the shapes you will be working with. Sacred geometry attributes a symbolic and sacred meaning to certain geometric shapes. The belief behind sacred geometry is that God or 'Source' is the supreme geometric architect. These geometric symbols are known, have names and are easily identifiable and...just may have magical properties.

Seeing a particular geometric shape can make you feel and think a different way. They can be used to shape an emotion or set a mood. Shapes can also create movement or depth to reach and change your mind's eye and thought. They may be able to be used for energetic protection or advancement of purpose. Seeing a shape in your dreams, having an affinity for a particular shape or even if you are drawn to a particular geometric shape may have an individual meaning or message meant expressly for you.

Your key geometric shape may give you clues to your purpose of why you are here on Earth at this time. It may represent your core values or core being. It can tell you the strengths you bring to this lifetime, or what you are meant to learn or achieve. Only you know how that geometric shape will resonate its meaning to you. Let's find out your key geometric shape.

DISCOVERY 1

Selecting Your Key Geometric Shape

Close your eyes and think of a shape. What did you see? Whatever geometric shape you saw or pictured in your mind's eye is your key geometric shape. Now refer to the Geometric Shape Meanings Chart to discover what your key geometric personality traits means. Then fill in your personal chart with your key Geometric Shape information.

Using Geometric Shapes for Protection and Advancement

There will be times in your life where you want to be energetically protected. Using white light to outline a geometric shape around you can infuse the qualities of that geometric shape to help protect you, or you can even use this method to help you accomplish what you desire. To do this look at the Geometric Shape Meanings Chart and select the shape you want or need for your protection or advancement of your goals. After selection do the following visualization.

Visualization

Find a comfortable place where you won't be distracted and stand up. Think of your intention. Now imagine a white, gold or silver light right above the top of your head. Watch as this line of light moves around your body outlining the geometric shape you chose. Watch as the line of light attaches itself back at the top of your head. Take a moment to feel the energy, the protection of this sacred geometric shape. Feel, know and trust that what you want to be accomplished will be accomplished. When you are ready open your eyes.

GEOMETRIC SHAPE MEANINGS

Shape	Meaning
Circle	Wholeness, Unity, Enlightenment, Perfection
Crescent	Creativity, Intuition
Cross	Communion, Harmony, Balance
Diamond	Creativity, Activation
Dot	Beginning
Hexagram	Strength, Protection, Healing, Balance
Lines - General Curved Diagonal Horizontal Vertical Zigzag	Division, Boundary Balance, Relief, Grace Excitement, Energy Peace, Rest, Tranquility Grandeur, Strength, Security Energy, Action, Movement
Octagon	Renewal, Justice, Spiritual Protection
Oval	Manifestation, Immortality
Parallelogram	Growth, Flexibility
Pentagram	Healing, Protection
Rectangle	Stability, Honesty, Order, Peace
Spiral	Expanding Energy, Evolution, Altered State
Square	Balance, Security, Dependable, Safe Place
Triangle	Power, Self-Discovery, Purpose

Tarot Cards

The Tarot is an 'ancient tradition' method performed with a pictorial deck of cards to gain insight into life questions and future revelations. There is speculation that Tarot cards started in Ancient Egypt, as well as by the Turks, Cathars, Sufis, Cabalists, Italians, French and more.

Historical data points that they came from Northern Italy, a couple of decades after playing cards fashioned after the Turkish Malmuk cards were brought to Europe by the Arabs around 1375 to 1378. The Marseilles French Deck, which is the card deck most people are familiar with, commenced around 1480. The first esoteric reference to Tarot cards was found in 1621 published in *The Fame and Confessions of the Rosicrucians*. The head of the Golden Dawn wrote a manuscript about the attributes of the Tarot in 1887 and things have been written about the Tarot until the present day.

Today the Tarot comes in many kinds and forms. As with all divination knowing the energy behind the tools is imperative for safe and effective use. The Tarot charts below gives you known and little known information about the Tarot. They include the qualities, life cycle, music, chakra, astrology, planet, archetype and meanings of all twenty-two cards.

DISCOVERY 1

For a quick divination you can try this method anytime you want. Place the **Tarot 2 Chart** in front of you. In your mind decide on a question. Now close your eyes and run your hands down the chart. When you feel heat or energy coming from the page, place your finger on the spot. Open your eyes and read the meaning in the chart to give you insight into your question.

TAROT 1

Card #		Qualities	Life Cycle	Music Note
0	The Fool	Origin/End, Chaos, Contingency, Impulse	Embryo	E
1	The Juggler	Will. Creativity, Intuition	Childhood	E
2	High Priestess	Body Healing, Wisdom, Mystery	Childhood	G Sharp A Flat
3	Empress	Earthiness, Nature, Fecundity	Childhood	F Sharp G Flat
4	Emperor	Masculine Mind, Will, Direction	Childhood	C
5	High Priest	Soul Healing, Self-Discovery, Understanding	Childhood	C Sharp D Flat
6	The Lovers	Society, Morality, Bestow or Confer Rights	Childhood	D
7	The Chariot	Power, Intellect, Self-Confidence	Childhood	D Sharp E Flat
8	Justice	Reason, Balance of Will	Childhood	F Sharp G Flat
9	The Hermit	Isolation, Rootlessness, Stoic Wisdom	Childhood	F
10	Wheel of Fortune	Ideal Form, Chance, Fate	Childhood	A Sharp B Flat
11	Strength	Nature Tamer, Power, Miracle	Childhood	E
12	Hanged Man	Sacrifice, Patient Virtue, Harden Will	Childhood	G Sharp A Flat
13	Death	Transformation	Adolescent	G
14	Temperance	Personified Virtue, Supernatural	Adolescent	G Sharp A Flat
15	The Devil	Libido, Rebel Will	Adolescent	A
16	The Tower	End Blind Faith, Introspective, Thought	Adolescent	C
17	The Star	Mediation, Enlightenment	Adolescent	A Sharp B Flat
18	The Moon	Bound Spirit, Compromise, Illusion of Matter	Adolescent	B
19	The Sun	Joy, Hope, Freedom, Regained Innocence	Adolescent	D
20	Last Judgment	Future, Consciousness	Adolescent	C
21	The World	Eternity, Concrete Actuality	Adolescent	A

~ TAROT CARDS ~

TAROT 2

Card #	Chakra	Astrology Planets	Meaning	Archetype
0 The Fool	3rd Eye to Crown	Uranus	Face unknown, changing directions, unexpected	Dionysus, Cain, Orestes
1 The Juggler	3rd Eye to Crown	Mercury	New vitality, opportunities, intuitive power	Hermes, Adam
2 High Priestess	Heart to Crown	Moon	Mother Nature, Discovery of Inner Self, High Intuition	Moira, Isis, Diana
3 Empress	3rd Eye	Venus	Marriage, partnership, creativity	Aphrodite, Demeter,
4 Emperor	Navel to Solar	Aries	Evaluate, Reform, authority structure	Zeus, Thor, Jehovah
5 High Priest	Navel to Solar	Taurus	Religion, intelligence, metaphysics	He, The Breath
6 The Lovers	Throat to 3rd Eye	Gemini	Love or career choice	Dioscuri, Paris
7 The Chariot	Throat to 3rd Eye	Cancer	Balance, intelligence, control of passion	Ares
8 Justice	Heart to Throat	Libra	Make decision, give and take, balance perception	Athena, Pallas
9 The Hermit	Head to Throat	Virgo	Build foundation, patience, find higher need	Kronos, Buddha, Marcus Aurelius
10 Wheel of Fortune	Solar	Jupiter	Change of fate, growth	The Furies
11 Strength	Solar	Leo	Courage, strength, discipline	Hercules
12 Hanged Man	Solar to Throat	Neptune	Attitude, fantasy, prejudice	Prometheus
13 Death	Solar to Heart	Scorpio	Passage to cycle	Pluto, Judas
14 Temperance	Navel to Heart	Sagittarius	Access balance, adapting, relationship	Iris
15 The Devil	Solar to Heart	Capricorn	Unnecessary ties to material world, confront other side	Pan, Cerebrus
16 The Tower	Solar to Heart	Mars	Storm before calm, disruption through intellect	King Minos
17 The Star	Heart to 3rd Eye	Aquarius	Hope, Inspiration, Health	Pandora
18 The Moon	Root to Solar	Pisces	Uncertainty, instinct, many meanings	Hecate
19 The Sun	Navel to Solar	The Sun	Worldly deeds, good relationship, trust, clarity	Aten, Apollo
20 Last Judgment	Root to Solar	Pluto	Spiritual awakening, renewal, conscious shift	Hestia, Hermes
21 The World	Solar to Navel	Saturn	Fulfillment, Harmony	Kali, Sophia

Tea Leaf Reading

Reading tea leaves is a method to answer questions and the future. Certain preparations are used to enable the reading of the tea leaf symbols. Symbols are then interpreted by the reader. Meanings and interpretations can vary. To help you start see Tea Leaf Reading Meanings chart.

Tea Cup Preparation

1) 1/2 teaspoon loose tea in cup, pour hot water, drink.
2) Leave small bit of water at bottom and swirl cup.
3) Rotate cup at an angle to slosh out water.
4) Turn cup over on paper towel in front of person.
5) Person rotates cup clockwise 3 times (cup is still turned over).
6) Turn cup right side up. Do reading.

Position of Tea Leaves
Read Clockwise
Look for Symbols.
2 Symbols 1/4" apart influence each other

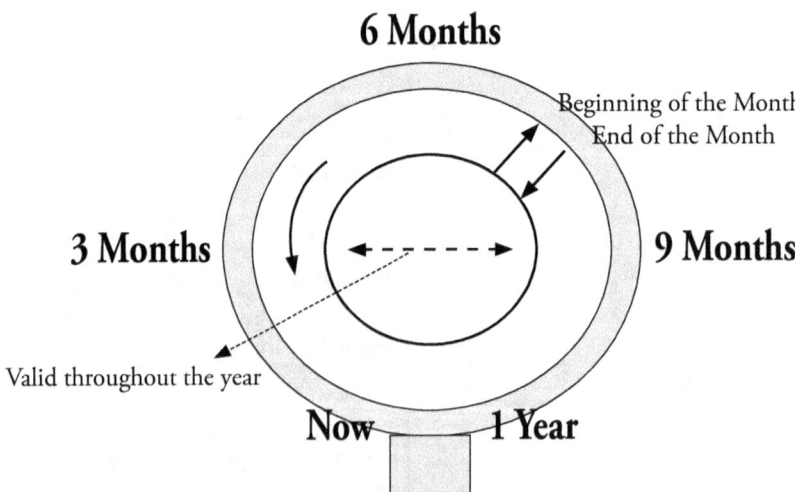

DISCOVERY

Using the 'Tea Cup Preparation' make a cup of loose tea. Look for a symbol, then refer to the Tea Leaf Meanings chart. This symbol represents something about you. Fill in your symbol chart.

TEA LEAF MEANINGS

Symbol	Meaning	Symbol	Meaning	Symbol	Meaning
Anchor	Unsettled Condition	Hand	Assistance	Ring	Marriage
Angel	Protection, Awareness	Hat	New Role	Rope	Capture
Ape	Mimic, Copy	Heart	Love	Seahorse	Family
Baby	New Venture or Start	Hills	Truth	Sheep Shoe	Passive
Balloon	Fun, Take Chance	Horseshoe	Good Luck	Shoe	Effort
Banana	Foreign Interaction	Jug	Party	Skeleton	A Secret
Bat	Treachery, Danger	Kettle	Guests	Spider	Good Luck
Bell	Announcement	Key	Success	Spoon	Training
Bird	Good Message	Knife	Fear	Stairs	Success
Blobs	Ordinary Next Year	Ladder	Success	Star	Success
Bottle	Temptation	Lamb	Kindness	Sun	Happiness
Cane	Temporary Illness	Lamp	Guidance	Table	Favor
Clouds	Temporary Problem	Leaf	Health	Tear Drop	Sorrow
Diamond	Jewelry, Gift	Money	Money	Telephone	Meeting
Dish	Invitation	Moon	Change	Telescope	Long Distance Call
Door	Opportunity	Mountain	Challenge	Torch	Sacrifice
Ear	Good News	Mouse	Pest	Tree	Family
Egg	Success	Music Note	Harmony	Truck	Hard work
Eye	Psychic Ability	Necktie	Conformity	Umbrella	Protection
Fish	Increased Wealth	Nest	Emotional Security	Vase	Secret Admirer
Flag	Maintain Integrity	Pig	Greed	Wall	Misunderstanding
Flowers	Compliments	Pipe	Reconciliation	Whale	Worry Over Nothing
Fool	New Experience	Power Lines	Great Resources	Wine Glass	Party
Fork	Assistance	Rabbit	Carefree	Worm	Humility
Glass	Dissatisfaction	Rainbow	Easy Going	Wishbone	Sorrow
Gun	Anger	Rake	Search	Wreath	Wish Granted

Trees

Trees are ancient cognizant beings. They talk, support and nourish each other through their root systems. Trees are very prevalent in mythology, legends and the Bible. They symbolize life, wisdom, strength, endurance, nourishment, healing, transformation and power. Trees are also the synthesis of earth, water, heaven and have witnessed the evolution of the planet and all things on it. There is also the Tree of Life which is sacred and symbolizes a connection to everything.

One of the magically important things about trees is how they can interact with you. They can inspire you to express and manifest love, gratitude, healing, kindness, friendship and happiness. It is almost limitless in how trees can help and even protect you. It is important to remember that trees contain ancient knowledge and need to be treated with knowledge and respect. Here are some ways to allow the blessings and power of trees into your life.

Visualization
Selecting Your Power Tree

Close your eyes, and concentrate on the breath and breathe in deeply. Breathe rhythmically in and out, then close your eyes and imagine you are in a grove of trees. There are all different types and kinds of trees. You feel happy and energized. You slowly turn in a circle and take in all the energies of the trees surrounding you in the grove. You feel a pull and a subtle energy of one particular tree. Turn to face this tree and the energy the tree is sending you gets stronger. Walk over to the tree and hug it. Feel the tree's energy join with you. Step back from the tree and look at its bark. In the bark the name of the tree appears. Remember it. This tree has an affinity for you for all of your life. Say thank you to the tree and welcome it in you as your friend. Now open your eyes and fill in your personal symbol chart with your Power Tree name.

DISCOVERY
Consulting Tree Wisdom

If you need help or answers from the tree realm you can ask the trees. Refer to the 'Tree Meanings' Chart below. Select the Tree and its meaning that is closest to what your desired outcome is. Either find a live tree or meditate with or without an image of that tree. Ask the tree if it will respectfully help you. Touch its trunk, branch or leaf and be open to the exchange of energies or messages as they are given to you. Remember to thank the tree when you are done.

~ TREES ~

Visualization
Using Tree Power for Balance and Protection

Choose a tree from the chart below. Close your eyes, and concentrate on the breath and breathe in deeply. Imagine you are in a beautiful, sunny place and the tree is before you. The sky is the perfect blue. The air temperature is exactly right for you. A branch of the tree reaches out to you. Smiling you reach out and gently hold the branch. There is no fear and you feel peace. You feel your feet become like roots of the tree and go deep towards the center of the earth. Still holding the branch your arms reach up towards the sky. They reach far up through the sky and your head is in the clouds. You may even reach beyond the Universe to the Source of Life itself. You feel centered and balanced with your feet in the ground and your head in the clouds. Feel the energy going through you. Balancing you. Healing you. The energy is amazing. You feel your uniqueness as part of the whole. You feel happy, centered and balanced. As you hold on to the trees branch you feel a Light come from Source surrounding you. At the same time you feel and see the Light energy essence of the tree coming through the branch you are holding in your hand. The tree's Light mingles with the Light from Source that is surrounding your body. You know this Light protects you. Absorb the feeling and feel the Light protecting you for as long as you need. Feeling Balanced, Happy, Whole and Protected when you are ready open your eyes.

TREE MEANINGS

Tree	Meaning	Tree	Meaning
Almond	Alertness, Rebirth	Holly	Love, Protection
Apple	Happiness, Healing	Honeysuckle	Intuition, Change
Ash	Adaptability, Psychic Protection	Lemon	Purification.
Aspen	Fearlessness, Communication	Magnolia	Alignment
Beech	Prosperity, Tolerance	Maple	Unconditional Love, Balance
Birch	Healing, Fertility	Oak	Strength. Long Life,
Cedar	Emotional Balance, Strength	Olive	Clarity, Knowledge, Victory
Cherry	Insight, Riches	Orange	Good Fortune, Pure Love
Cottonwood	Patience, Resiliency	Palm	Peace, Protection
Cypress	Understanding, Happiness	Peach	Marriage, Wealth
Elder	Protection, Healing	Pear	Transience, Delicacy
Elm	Strength, Intuition	Pine	Cleansing, Emotion Balance
Eucalyptus	Psychic Growth, Cleansing	Sycamore	Beauty, Nourishment
Fig	Knowledge, Enlightenment	Walnut	Transition, Hidden Wisdom
Hawthorne	Growth, Creativity	Willow	Flexibility, Healing
Hazel	Hidden Wisdom	Yew	Immortality

Water

Water is one of the essences of life. It is not inert but a living substance that has emotions and reactions. One of the most complex symbols water has been used at the center of spirituality and religious rituals all over the world. The movement of water is ever-changing and varies from being strong and fluid to gentle and stagnant. It has layers of currents and undercurrents. More than most other symbols water has a wide range of meanings. The one thing it symbolizes is constant change. Water symbolizes birth and is known as the Mother of Creation and represents life, regeneration and renewal. It has many meanings for you and can represent your spiritual or emotional state. Working with water is very powerful.

DISCOVERY

Discovering Your Water Symbol

When you think of water what first comes to mind? What type of water do you envision? For a moment think of all the kinds of water that exist: brooks, creeks, ponds, lakes, rivers, seas, oceans and glaciers. Where do you see yourself where you feel the most stress free, calm and empowered? Think about this and when you have selected your water source look at the 'Water Meaning' chart and discern its meaning. Now think how this meaning applies to your life. This is your Water Symbol. Write the name and meaning down in your personal symbol chart.

Visualization
Working With Water

Look at the chart and select the type water and its meaning that is closest to your goal. State the intention you have out loud. Find a relaxing place and uncross your arms and legs as you get comfortable. Close your eyes, and concentrate on the breath and breathing. Breathe deeply. Imagine you are near or under your selected water source. The movement is a gentle energy. This is your private place where no one can enter take off your clothes and allow the water to flow over you. It cleanses you and makes the vision that you want incredibly clear. The water clears away any negativity. It is healing you. Soothing you. It energizes you. Now the water becomes stronger and more forceful but you are not afraid. You feel it shifting you.

Changing you. Transforming you so that you can activate and achieve your goal. The water changes again in a repetitive rhythmic pattern. Strong and then gentle. Over and Over and Over again. Listen as the water tells you how to accomplish what you want. One by one you are getting focus and understanding to achieve your goal. Your focus becomes clear and you are shown that that being steadfast in what you learned when navigating this water will help you achieve your goal. Now watch as the water flows over every part of your body. It is gentle as it surrounds your body and goes into every cell of your body — cleansing you from negativity. Protecting you. Transforming you. All to help you achieve your goal. The water subsides and you find that you are dry. Put on your clothes look at the source of water and feel your power, determination, clarity and purpose. You feel healed, happy and protected. You know that you are ready to achieve your goal. Saying thank you to the water, when you are ready open your eyes.

WATER MEANINGS

Water Type	Meaning
Brook	Wisdom
Creek	Timelessness
Flood	Excessive Emotion
Fountain	Spiritual Energy
Glaciers	Aloofness, Melting Past Grievances
Groundwater	Change, Transformation
Lake	Collective Wisdom
Ocean	Consciousness
Pool	Freshness, Relaxation
Rain	Spiritual Cleansing, Growth
River	Spiritual Journey, Destiny
Waterfall	Positive Energy, Freedom
Well	Healing Power
Saltwater	Healing, Protection
Seas	Memory, Truth
Stream	Balance

BONUS
HEALTH & AWARENESS CHARTS

Acupressure: Points & Applications

According to Eastern Tradition energy, called Qi, is believed to flow through the body in specific paths. When a blockage occurs in these energy paths it inhibits or stops the flow of energy which then can result in illness or mental disorders.

Acupuncture uses very fine hair-like needles that are placed into specific energy points on the body to displace or disperse the energy blockage. Acupressure is slightly different. It is when you simply apply pressure, instead of needles, to an associated 'energy point.' This can be very effective especially when you use essential oils in the process. In some circumstances the aromatherapy oil can take the place of the acupuncture needles but even simple acupressure without oils can be effective. If you want to use essential oils refer to Chapter 5 in this book.

Before you do a treatment make sure you have the time and a peaceful place where you can stay focused. The illustrations in the following pages show you the Major Points from the Front and Back View of the Body.

Once a point has been confidently located then it is time to apply firm, even, steady pressure on that specific point. The pressure used should not be to the point of excruciating pain but does need to be great enough to feel a sensation. Remember there should never be bruising.

The length of time to use acupressure on a point is dependent on personal experience but normally 7, 10 or 30 seconds should work in most cases. You can also use acupressure as many times as you need and as often as you want. Always listen to the feedback of your own body or the person you are working on.

Each ailment has specific points associated to an ailment which helps remove the blockage and restore energy flow. Research on your own if you want more detailed information.

ACUPRESSURE POINTS: FRONT

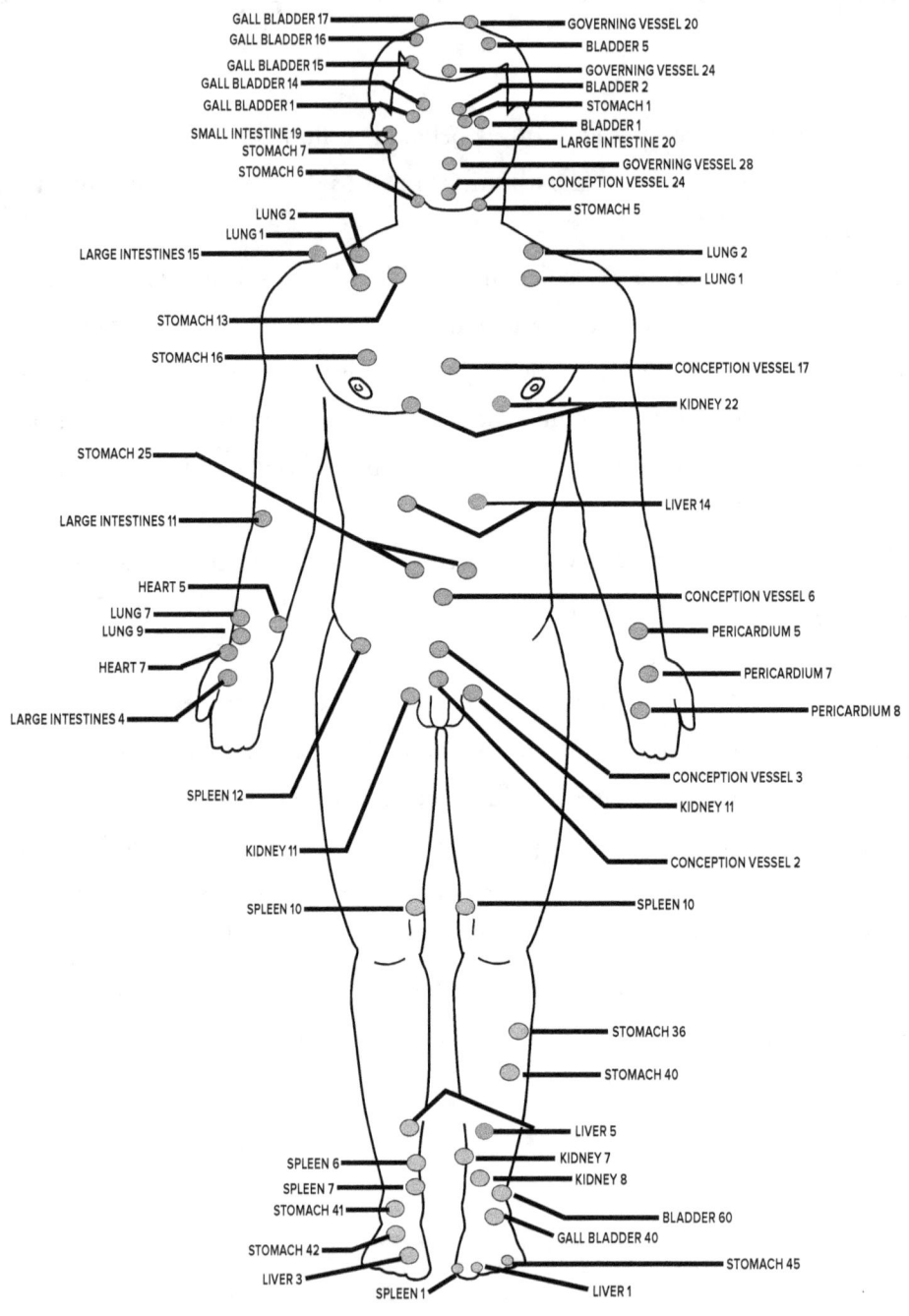

ACUPRESSURE POINTS: BACK

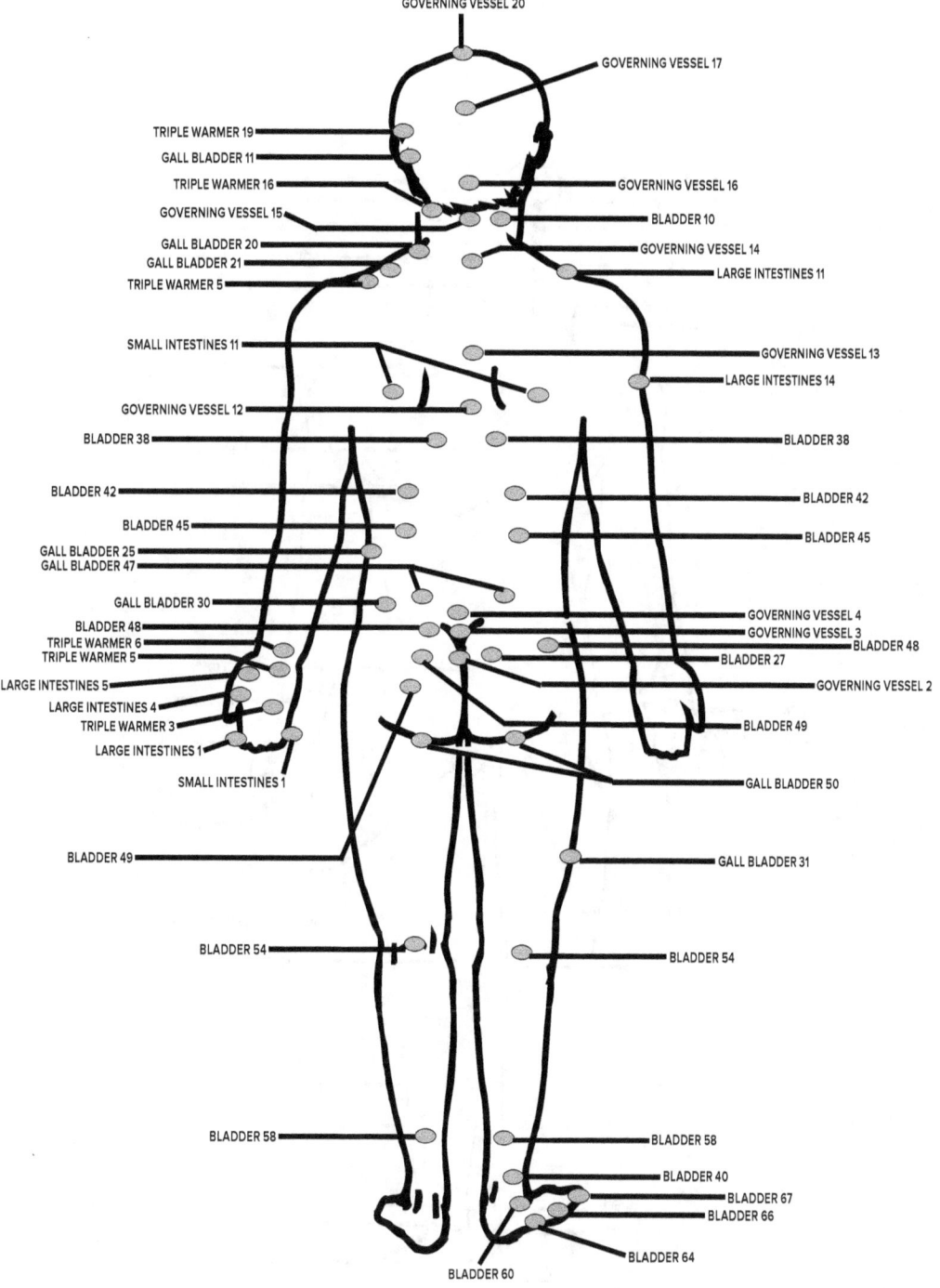

~ SYMBOLS OF YOU ~

ACUPRESSURE APPLICATIONS

According to Eastern tradition if you apply pressure on the appropriate point for 7 - 10 - 30 seconds, symptoms can be relieved and energy balance is restored. The illustration and chart below give you the related healing points and common ailment applications.

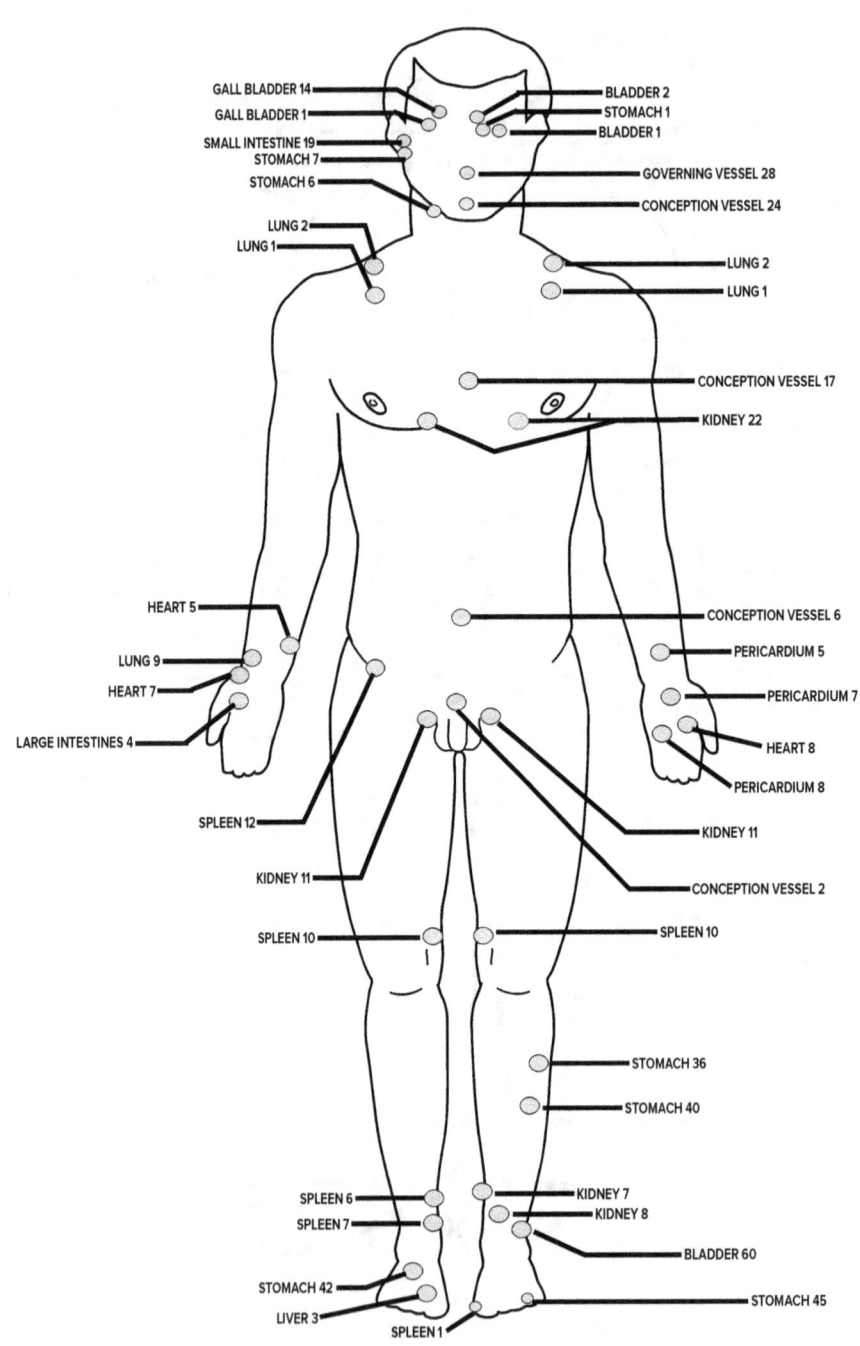

ACUPRESSURE APPLICATION CHART

Symptom	Acupressure Points
Anxiety	Heart 5, 7; Lung 1, 2; Stomach 42; Spleen 3
Asthma	Bladder 38, Conception Vessel 17; Lung 1, 2
Back Pain	Bladder 38, 45, 48; Governing Vessel 2, 4; Heart 3, 8
Bladder	Bladder 60, 64, 66, 67
Claustrophobia	Heart 5, 7, 8, 9; Lung 1, 2; Pericardium 5, 8; Stomach 43; Spleen 3
Congestion	Bladder 48, Conception Vessel 17; Lung 1, 2
Conjunctivitis (pink eye)	Bladder 1, 2; Gall Bladder 1; Liver 3; Stomach 1; Spleen 7
Constipation	Large Intestine 4
Depression	Heart 5, 7, 8, 9; Kidney 1*; Large Intestine 1; Lung 1, 2; Pericardium 8; Stomach 40, 45*
Ear Discomfort	Bladder 64; Kidney 1*;
Fatigue	Kidney 1*, 3, 11, 22; Stomach 36
Fever	Bladder 66; Heart 7; Kidney 8; Pericardium 7; Small Intestines 4; Triple Warmer 4
Gas	Lung 1, 9; Stomach 45; Spleen 3
Gout	Lung 1, 2; Stomach 42; Spleen 1*, 3
Headache: Front	Bladder 2; Gall Bladder 1, 14; Governing Vessel 4; Stomach 6; Triple Warmer 23
Headache: Sides	Gall Bladder 4, 20; Small Intestines 19; Stomach 6, 7; Triple Warmer 23
Headache: Back	Gall Bladder 19, 20; Governing Vessel 17; Triple Warmer 16, 19
Heartburn	Stomach 42; Spleen 4
Herpes	Spleen 7
Hot Flashes	Bladder 66; Kidney 3; Stomach 42; Triple Warmer 3
Impotence	Conception Vessel 2; Governing Vessel 14; Heart 7, 9; Kidney 1, 3, 7, 11; Pericardium 8; Triple Warmer 1
Insomnia	Heart 7, 9; Kidney 3, 8; Lung 1
Menstrual Cramps	Conception Vessel 2; Stomach 36, 42; Spleen 3, 46, 10, 12
Nausea	Stomach 42; Spleen 3
Sore Throat	Conception Vessel 24;
Prostate	Bladder 64; Conception Vessel 6; Heart 1, 3;
Shock	Conception Vessel 17; Heart 7, 9; Kidney 1*, Lung 1, 2; Pericardium 5
Stress	Conception Vessel 17; Heart 7, 9; Lung 1, 2; Small Intestines 10*; Stomach 42
Toothache	Governing Vessel 28
Vomiting	Stomach 42; Spleen 3
*Not To Be Used When Pregnant	

Cabala (Kabbalah, Qabalah)

In a faction of the Jewish religion the Kabbalah is considered to be the Tree of Life and is used in various traditions as a mystical force or guide. The Cabala diagram sketches out a blueprint of how life may be experienced. The diagram is also used by Hermetic Qabalah, Christian Cabala, Theosophy and others.

The origin of the Kabbalah is said to have come from God. It was passed down to Adam then to Noah, Abraham and Moses. The Cabala is very near to the Christian Gnosticism.

There are three columns, ten Sephirah (also known as nodes or spheres) and twenty two lines that form the Tree of Life. The three vertical columns (also known as Pillars) are named: The Pillar of Severity, The Pillar of Equilibrium (or Balance) and the Pillar of Mercy. In these vertical columns are the Sephirah which have similar characteristics. Viewed from top to bottom the Sephirah are attributes of God. However, viewed from bottom to top they also represents a physical and/or spiritual characteristic of man. The ten Sephirah, or nodes, is where Energy is said to flow from the top to the bottom of the Tree. Balance of the Sephirah is really the basis of the Tree of Life. The twenty two lines that connect to the Sephirah are the paths of Life.

The Cabala can be considered walking the path to your highest Spirituality, as well as being used as practical guide to help you through your life. For centuries Cabalistic principles have held a healing potential for your body, mind, emotions and spirit. The Tree of life is also believed to be the pathway to eternal life and a way to heaven.

The Tarot is influenced by the Hermetic Order of the Golden Dawn who's teaching strongly links Tarot to the teachings of Kabbalah. There are twenty two paths of the Tree of life, one for each letter of the Hebrew alphabet and there are 22 major tarot cards that are also associated with the Kabbalah. Do your own research to fully know and use the Cabala.

~ CABALA (KABBALAH, QABALAH) ~

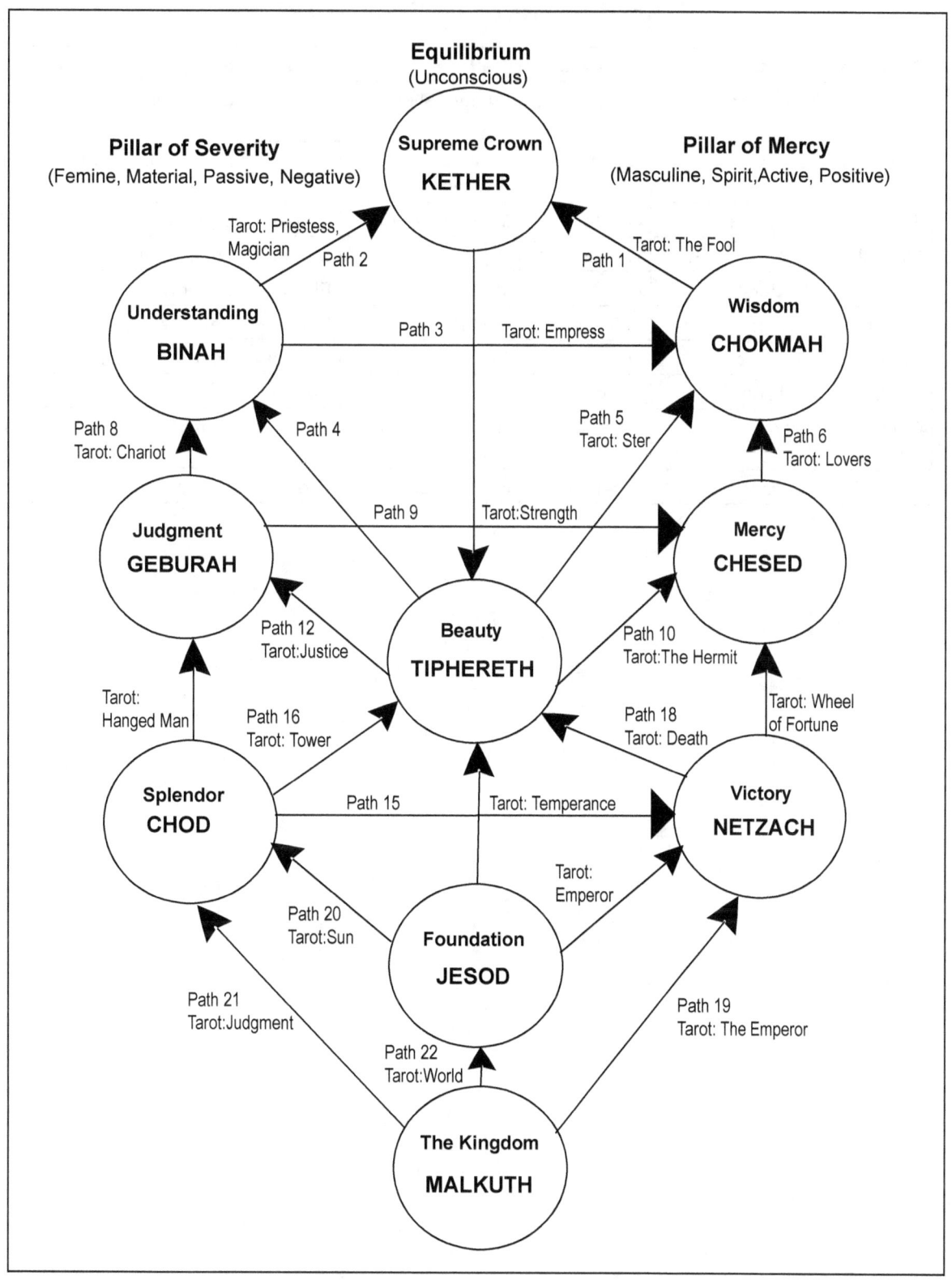

CABALA: TREE OF LIFE CHART

Sephirah	Source	Body Part	Trait	Color	Pillar	Planet
Kether	Supreme Crown	Head	Primordial Force	White	Equilibrium	
Tiphereth	Beauty	Chest	Universal Awareness	Yellow	Equilibrium	Sun
Jesod	Foundation	Genitals	Material World	Purple	Equilibrium	Moon
Malkuth	The Kingdom	Whole Body	Physical	Brown	Equilibrium	
Binah	Understanding	Heart	Intelligence	Black	Severity	Saturn
Geburah	Judgment	Left Arm	Power	Red	Severity	Mars
Chod	Splendor	Left Leg	Glory	Orange	Severity	Mercury
Chokma	Wisdom	Brain	Enlightenment	Silver	Mercy	
Chesed	Mercy	Right Arm	Greatness, Love, Truth	Blue	Mercy	Jupiter
Netzach	Victory	Right Leg	Eternal Form	Green	Mercy	Venus

Cheyenne Medicine Wheel

In Native American Tradition the Cheyenne Medicine Wheel depicts the Wheel of Life. Everyone walks the wheel of life to raise consciousness, gain power and facilitate growth. The Cheyenne Medicine Wheels can be built from stone on large plots of land on sacred spiritual sites or represented in art. There is a Cheyenne Medicine Wheel in the Big Horn mountain range that was built about 200 years ago, and is located directly over one of the ten sites in the world where ancient volcanoes formed the first and oldest layers of rock on Earth. Although still a mystery, the origin of this wheel has archaeological evidence that show Native American tribes have used that area for over 7,000 years.

The Energy Centers of the Wheel are the Four Directions. Each of the four directions on the medicine has its own significance. The Meanings of the Four Directions are interpreted differently by each tribe. However, each of the Four Directions (East, South, West, and North) is typically represented by a distinctive color and attributes given to the directions by the particular tribe. It can include the four seasons, the four stages of life (birth/childhood, youth/adolescence, adult/parenthood, elders/death), the four aspects of life (spiritual, intellectual, emotional, physical) and the four elements of nature.

The circle or wheel shape circle acknowledges the connectedness of everything in life and the continuous cycle of both the seen and unseen. It is said in the Crow traditions that vision quests were held either held actually in the medicine wheel or close by one. The Cheyenne Medicine Wheel can show us our way back to our center and to health, as well as, our connection to all things and our spiritual path home. The Cheyenne Medicine Wheel is also a way of creating sacred space and calling forth nature's healing energies.

CHEYENNE MEDICINE WHEEL

RAISES AWARENESS, POWER & GROWTH EXPERIENCES

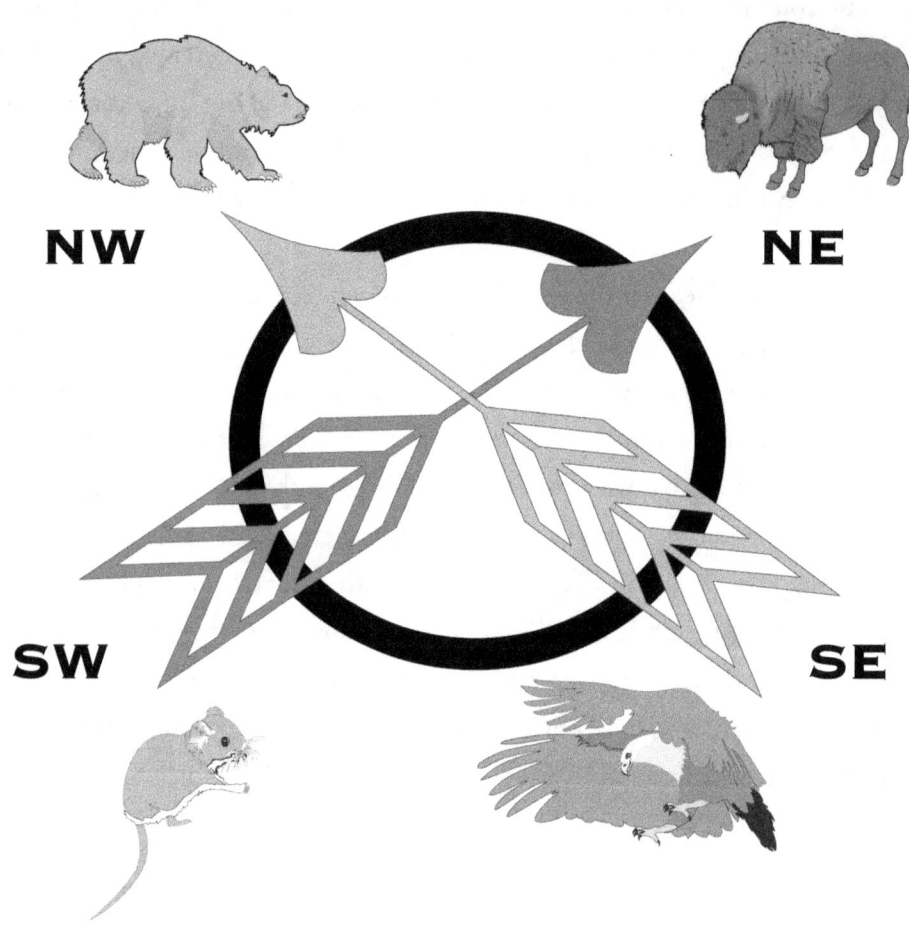

CHEYENNE MEDICINE WHEEL CHART

Direction	Color	House	Element	Abode	Source
Northeast	Black	Buffalo		Dog Soldiers	Power, Death Wisdom, Disease, Silence
East	Yellow Blue		Air	Men's Lodge	Past, Mental
Southeast	White	Eagle		Peace Chiefs	Light, Life, Renewal, Illumination
South	Red, Green		Fire	War Chiefs	Present, Physical
Southwest	Red	Mouse		Singers, Storytellers, Mediums Healers	Growth, Weather, Innocence
West	Black, Brown		Water	Women's Lodge	Future, Emotional
Northwest	Yellow	Bear		Council Lodge	Harvest Introspection, Perfection
North	Purple Sky Blue		Earth	Hunters Gatherers	Spiritual Transformation

Chinese Elements

The Chinese Elements are the forces of Nature that can be expressed as a primary influence on all of life. Comprised of five elements the Wu Xing. philosophy appeared between 770–476 B.C. The Five Element philosophy influences Chinese medicine, philosophy, feng shui, fortune-telling and the martial arts.

These five elements, which are wood, fire, earth, metal and water, are believed to make up the basis of everything on Earth and in the Universe. All the different elements are equally important, interconnected and belong to either the yin (male) or the yang (female) signs. In the Five Element Theory the Five Elements also generate interactions and characterize the life cycle of Birth, Initiation, Love, Rest and Death. In addition, each of these elements have their own associations and characteristics with certain aspects of nature. The elements produce basic interactions that includes the concepts that: Wood fuels fire. Fire forms Earth (e.g., volcanoes). Earth contains Metal. Metal carries Water (e.g., bucket). Water feeds Wood (e.g., trees).

When there is a negative interaction, or hostility, between the elements this creates negative energy, hardship and negativity. There are five interactions that can overcome this negative energy and restore balance. These are: Fire melts Metal. Metal penetrates Wood (e.g., sawing wood). Wood separates Earth (e.g., tree roots). Earth absorbs Water, Water quenched Fire.

The Chinese Five Elements are also associated with the 12 signs of the Chinese (Oriental) Zodiac. Each sign has the five elements directing their lives.

In Chinese philosophy good Feng Shui brings good luck. In every direction there is life force energy called Qi, and every direction is ruled by one of the five elements. So if you align yourself with getting the most Qi this can bring easy living and good luck. Feng Shui, or the art of placement, is meant to keep Qi energy flowing. To do this Feng Shui uses the five elements in specific positions.

CHINESE ELEMENT CHART 1

Element	Season	Direction	Relation	Planet
Water	Winter	North	Death	Mercury
Fire	Summer	South	Initiation	Mars
Wood	Spring	East	Birth	Jupiter
Metal	Autumn	West	Repose	Venus
Earth		Center	Love	Saturn

CHINESE ELEMENT CHART 2

Element	Coloe	Animal	Keywords	Qualities
Water	Black	Tortoise	Intelligence, Change, Communication	Rest Relaxation
Fire	Red	Phoenix	Energy Stimulation	Wellbeing Self Esteem
Wood	Green	Dragon	Innovative Creativity	Inner Vision Creativity
Metal	White	Tiger	Valor, Business, Conflict	Material and Spiritual Needs
Earth	Yellow	Dragon	Stability	Balance Perspective

CHINESE ELEMENT CHART 3

Element	Body Part	Acupressure Meridians	Energy Attributes	Regulates
Water	Kidneys Bladder	Kidneys, Bladder	Stores Energy Reserves	Body Fluids, Bones, Hearing, Memory
Fire	Heart Pericardium	Small Intestines, Triple Warmer	Energy Presence	Blood Circulation Emotional System
Wood	Gall Bladder	Liver	Inner Vision Creativity	Anger
Metal	Large Intestines, Lungs	Large Intestines, Lungs	Releases Unnecessary Energy	Breathing, Emotional Balance
Earth	Stomach	Spleen	Balances Physical and Emotional Energy	Compassion, Sexual Dysfunction, Digestion

Chinese Herbs

Chinese Herbalism is part of **Traditional Chinese Medicine (TCM)** which is at least 23 centuries old and Chinese herbal remedies date back at least 2,200 years. The herbs and herbal formulas were carried down by oral tradition and the earliest known written record of Chinese medicine is from the 3rd century B.C.

Various Chinese herbs and herbal components are a way to create a healing effect that goes beyond the physical properties of the herbs. The TCM practitioner chooses an herbal formula for their signature energy vibrations and adjusts the formula to a person's own unique body energy to achieve harmony in the body, support good health and strengthen organ function.

Chinese communities base their decisions about using herbal medicines on professional TCM doctors and practitioners, family traditions, Chinese apothecary store recommendations and by self-medication.

Herbal formulas are often created to be taken as an herbal tea and herbs that are targeted for specific conditions and may have specific times of the day to take the dose. It may take 2-3 days or up to 2-3 weeks to notice an improvement in your symptoms dependent on the seriousness of your illness. Do your own research and always check with your TCM practitioner to see what herbs are right for you. As a rule of thumb if you are taking western medicine or over-the-counter drugs you should take your Chinese herbal formula 1-2 hours apart. Plus you should avoid cold, raw, spicy, and oily foods, or foods that are difficult to digest and avoid drinking ice water, cold drinks, or acidic juices at the same time when taking the herbal formula.

CHINESE HERBS CHART 1

Name	Part Used	Used For:
Aconite Fu Tzu	Root	Sexual Potency, Flatulence, Pain, Arthritis, Numbness, Excess Moisture
Apricot Seed Ku Xing Ren	Kernel	Lungs, Large Intestines
Astragalus Huang Chi	Root	Increases energy, Diuretic, Spleen, Kidneys, Blood, Builds Immune System
Bupleurum Ch'Ai Hu	Root	Liver, Dizziness, Anxiety, Muscle Tone
Chrysanthemum Chu Ha	Flowers	Dizziness, Fever, Headaches, Blood, Eyes, Liver
Citrus Peet Chen Pi	Peel	Indigestion, Diarrhea, Vomiting, Colds, Abdominal Pain, Energy Circulation
Deer Antler Lu Rong	Cross Section of Antler	Hormone System, Aphrodisiac
Don Quai	Root	Menstruation, Cramps, Anemia, Insomnia, Constipation
Don Sen Tang Shen	Root	Increases Energy, Pancreas, Spleen, Infection, Diabetes, Inflammation
Eleuthero	Root Leaves	Insomnia, Bronchitis, Heart Disease, Lowers Cholesterol and Blood Pressure
Ephedra Ma Huang	Stems Branches	Congestion, Coughs, Flu, Fevers, Asthma, Adrenals
Fu Ling	Whole Fungus	Diuretic, Emotional Imbalance, Lung, Congestion, Insomnia, Spleen, Stomach
Gelatin	Hides of Black Donkeys	Blood, Hormones, Liver
Ginseng Jen Shen	Root	Whole Body, Heart, Blood Pressure, Circulation, Inflammation, Fever
Honeysuckle Yin Hua	Flowers	Detoxifier, Poison Ivy, Rashes, Flu
Ho Shou Wu Fo Ti	Root	Energy, Strength, Fertility Diabetes, Liver, Kidney, Blood, Hypoglycemia
Jujube Date Da T'sao	Whole Date	Energy, Forgetfulness, Dizziness, Insomnia, Stomach, Spleen, Pancreas
Licorice Gan T'sao	Root	Whole Body, Adrenals, Ulcers, Colds, Flu, Liver, Blood Detoxifier
Longan Berries Long Yen Rou	Berries	Women's Reproductive Organs, Anemia, Forgetfulness, Heart, Pancreas
Lycii Gay Gee	Berries	Fevers, Bronchitis, Kidneys, Liver, Colds, Cloudy Vision, Blood Purifier
Pay Shoo	Root	Diuretic, Indigestion, Diarrhea, Edema, Stomach, Pancreas, Kidneys

CHINESE HERBS CHART 1 *(cont.)*

Name	Part Used	Used For:
Peony Shoo-Yao	Root	Liver, Skin Eruptions, Infections, Cramps, Uterus, Anemia
Platy Odon Jive Gang	Root	Lungs, Sore Throat, Asthma, Bronchitis, Pneumonia
Pueraria Kuzu Root	Root	Gastrointestinal, Colds, Flu
Rehmannia Sok Day- Sang Day	Root	Blood Purifier, Bones, Tendons, Anemia, Fatigue, Weak Heart, Kidneys
Salvia Dang Shen	Root	Menses Regulation, Blood Tonic, Itch, Rheumatism, Abdominal Extension,
Scutellaria Huang Chi	Root	Nerves, Large Intestines, Heart, Gall Bladder, Liver, Lungs
Sileris Fang-Feng	Root	Chills, Joint Pain, Headache, Numbness, Tetanus
Tienchi	Root	Hemorrhage, Heart, Circulation, Fatigue, Stress, Wounds, Stomach
Wild Ginger Xi Xin	Root	Energy, Congestion, Spasms

Dice Fortune Telling

The method for using Dice for divination was used for centuries in India and China. Dice were said to originate from Egypt and used for divination there. Rome and Iran also used dice for fortune telling and gaming. Dice allows you to access your subconscious mind to help you disclose answers about your life and future. Here are two methods.

CIRCLE TOSS FOR QUESTIONS

1. Draw a 12 inch Diameter Circle
2. Think of your question and toss 3 Die within the Circle
3. Add all the numbers of the dice together and look up the meanings below

In Addition: If a die lands outside the circle it is considered unlucky. If a all dice land outside the circle retoss the dice but if all dice land outside again — STOP!

CIRCLE TOSS FOR QUESTIONS - MEANINGS

Value	Meaning	Value	Meaning
3	Unexpected Good News, A Gift	11	Unhappiness
4	Disappointment, Bad Luck	12	Good News
5	Wish Fulfilled	13	Grief, Worry
6	Financial Loss, Dishonest Friend or Loved One	14	New Friend or Admirer
7	Setbacks, Guard Your Secrets	15	Caution, Avoid Arguments
8	Strong Outside Forces	16	A Good Journey
9	Luck In Love, Reconciliation	17	Change
10	Domestic Happiness, Business Promotion	18	Success, Advancement, Wealth

CIRCLE TOSS FOR FUTURE REVELATIONS

1. Draw a 12 inch diameter circle
2. Divide the circle into 12 equal segments
3. Write the letters A-L one to a segment
4. Shake and toss 3 of the Dice into the circle
5. Look and note the Segment and number of each Die
6. Now look at the chart for the meaning.

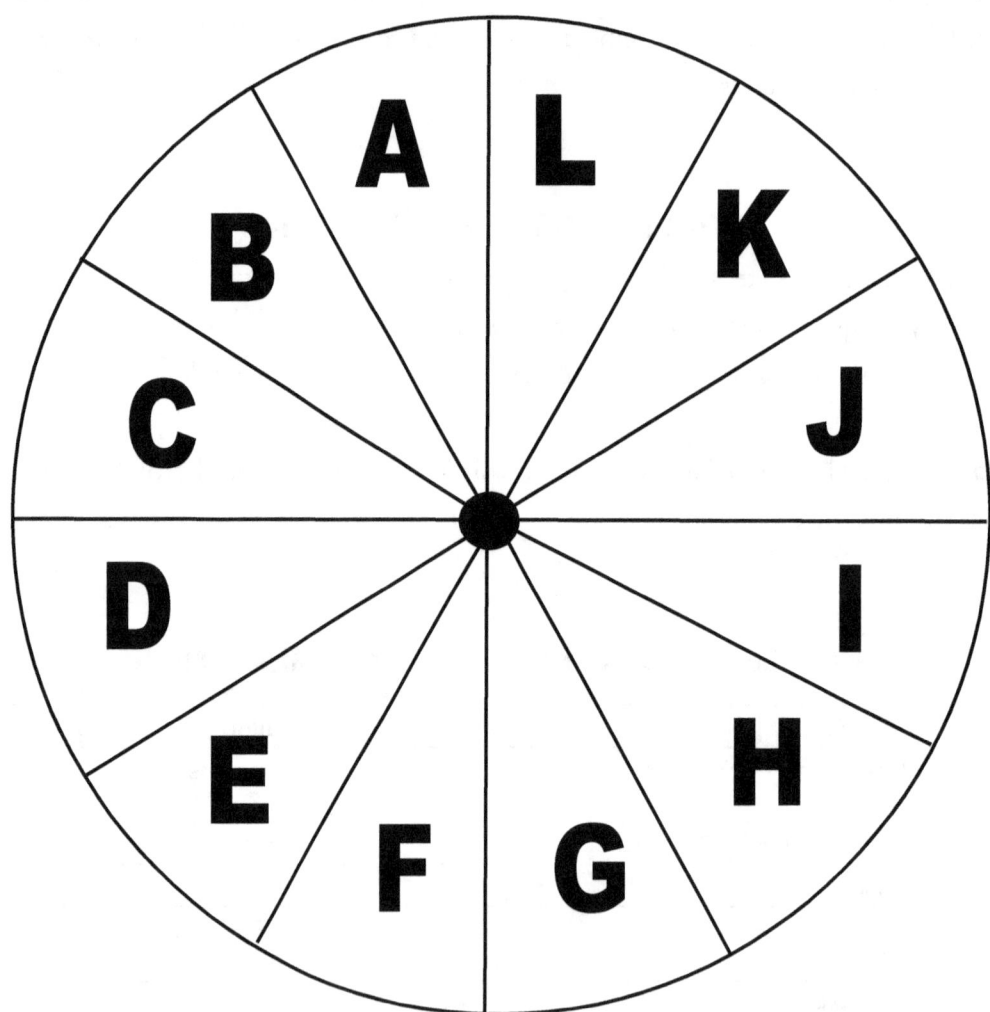

CIRCLE TOSS - FUTURE REVELATION MEANINGS

Board Segment	Meaning	Dice Number	Meaning
A	Next Year	1	Favorable Relate to Other Dice
B	Finances	2	Success Depends On Friends
C	Travel	3	Excellent for Success
D	Domestic Affairs	4	Disappointment, Difficulties
E	Present	5	Good Fortune
F	Health	6	Uncertainty
G	Love & Marriage		
H	Legal Matters		
I	Present Emotional State		
J	Career		
K	Friends		
L	Enemies		

Domino Fortune Telling

Dominoes are descendants of the six sided dice, and although a very similar game was played in ancient Egypt, the domino appears to have been invented independently in Europe and China. An ancient tradition in China since the 12th century, Domino Fortune Telling was and is used to give answers about life questions and provide a look into what the future might hold.

DOMINO FORTUNE TELLING METHOD

1. Shuffle dominoes face down and think of a question.
2. Choose 1st Domino. Turn it over. Refer to the Domino chart for its meaning.
3. Return Domino to the pile and reshuffle.
4. Select your 2nd Domino and repeat Steps 2 and 3.
5. Select your 3rd and last domino and repeat Steps 2 and 3.

Note: If the same tile is drawn twice your wish will be granted soon. An old legend says for a domino reading to be effective you should only do one wish per session and you should do only one session a week.

DOMINO MEANINGS

Domino	Meaning	Domino	Meaning
Six/Six	Happiness, Success, Prosperity in All	Four/Three	Happiness, Success
Six/Five	Patience and Tenacity	Four/Two	Setback or Loss, Beware of Deceitful Friend
Six/Four	Quarrel, Unsuccessful Law Suit	Four/One	Financial Problems, Pay Debts
Six/Three	Travel, A Gift, Enjoyment,	Four/Blank	Disappointment, Bad News
Six/Two	Good Luck for an Honest Person	Three/Three	Wedding, Good Finances
Six/One	End of a Problem, Wedding,	Three/Two	Good Change, Caution With Money
Six/Blank	Beware of a False Friend	Three/One	Answer Is No, Unexpected Useful News
Five/Five	Change Brings Success	Three/Blank	Unexpected Problem
Five/Four	Financial Luck But Avoid Investing Now	Two/Two	Success and Happiness
Five/Three	Beware of a False Friend	Two/One	Loss of Property or Money, Happy Social Life
Five/Two	Birth, Sociability, Enjoyment	Two/Blank	Travel and New Friends
Five/One	New Love Affair or Ending an Old Love Affair	One/One	Pleasure and Harmony, Make A Decision
Five/Blank	Sadness	One/Blank	Be Careful
Four/Four	Happiness, Celebration	Blank/Blank	Negative Aspects In All Areas

Herbs

Herbs are plants that contain medicinal properties and the practice of using these plants is called Herbalism. Since prehistoric times herbs have been used to facilitate healing in every culture on every continent on Earth. Passed down from healer to healer in the oral tradition the Sumerians gave us the first written record of herbs, found on a clay tablet in ancient Mesopotamia dating about 5,000 years ago. The pharmaceutical drug industry was originally based in trying to find and isolate the powerful ingredients in herbs. Herbs are part of Nature's pharmacy. It's interesting to note that Western Medicine, started in 1493-1541, pales by comparison to herbalism that has been used successfully for many millennia. As of the year 2000 the World Health Organization (WHO) 80% of the earth's population still relied on herbalism.

There are many ways to use herbs as therapy. Herbs therapies can be used to purify the blood and cleanse the lymphatic system to eliminate toxins. They can bring warmth, energy circulation and stimulation to the body. They can be used to take away pain, calm the mind and lift the spirit.

All parts of the plant may be used as a medicinal herb the flowers, leaves, stems and roots. Each of these parts may have different properties and even do different things.

You can use herbs by taking them internally as a capsule, tablet, powder, extract, tincture, syrup, infusion, vinegar, wine or tea. Externally herbs can be used as an oil, liniment, gargle, enema, douche, plasters, compress, bolus, poultice or bath.

Dosages are usually dependent on weight with larger doses going to heavier individuals while children, pregnant women and the elderly require smaller doses. During pregnancy a woman can respond differently to an herb than when she is not pregnant.

In using herbal therapies you must choose the herbs and preparation method that best suits the condition that is being treated. In making that choice you need to consider the age of the person, their lifestyle and the environment they live in. Remember herbs are plants and some people may be allergic to some and not to others.

There are some essential guidelines to be aware of if you plan to take herbs medicinally for self-care:
1. Knowledge is key to successful treatment and make no mistake herbs are natural medicine that need to be treated with knowledge and respect. When in doubt always check with your natural health care provider or herbalist.
2. Use the right herb and buy them from a reputable company.
3. Use only the recommended dosages for the recommended period of time.

4. Remember to use the correct part of the plant
5. Don't take herbs if you are pregnant, planning to become pregnant or nursing a baby without consulting your healthcare practitioner first.
6. If using an herbal remedy for the first time take a small dose to test for an allergic reaction.

When buying herbal remedies it is important that you buy from a viable source. If in doubt call the manufacturer and ask them how long they have been in business, how do they do quality control on their herbs and are they made in a pharmaceutical grade facility. Find out if they are a member of the American Herbal Products Association or other organization. Make sure you buy organically grown herbs.

The following charts are just some of the common herbs and only one thing they are known for. There may be in fact many different conditions associated with that herb. Research is key.

HERB CHART 1

Herb/Uses	Herb/Uses	Herb/Uses
Acorn: TB, Aids	Blue Cohash: Menses	Coltsfoot: Coughs
Agrimony: Astringent	Boneset: Colds, Flu	Comfrey: Healing
Aloe: Burns, Poison Ivy	Buchu: PMS	Corn Silk: Urinary Infection
Angelica: Arthritis	Buckthorn: Laxative	Coriander: Antiseptic
Anise: Menopause	Burdock: Food Poisoning	Cranberry: Urinary Infection
Asafoetida: Gas, Candida	Calendula: Ear Aches	Damania: Depression
Balm: Anxiety, Insomnia	Caraway: Digestion	Dandelion: Stomach
Barberry: Bronchitis	Cascara: Constipation	Dill: Abdominal Pain
Basil: Immune System	Catnip: Anxiety	Dusty Miller: Cloudy Vision
Bay Leaf: Anxiety	Celery Seed: Stress	Echinacea: Immune System
Barberry: Bronchitis	Chamomile: Digestion	Elecampane: Respiratory
Bayberry: Colds, Flu	Chapparal: Cancer	Ephedra: Hay Fever
BlackBerry: Fevers	Cinnamon: Anesthetic	Eucalyptus: Antiseptic
Black Cohash: Nerves	Clove: Parasitic	Evening Primrose: PMS
Black Haw: Menopause	Cocoa: Jet Lag	Fennel: Digestion
Bloodroot: Skin Cancer	Coffee: Decongestant	Fenugreek: Cholesterol

HERB CHART 2

Herb/Uses	Herb/Uses	Herb/Uses
Feverfew: Headache	Kava Kava: Fatigue	Mints: Coughs
Garlic: Antibiotic	Kelp: Antiseptic, Energy	Mistletoe: Healing
Gentian: Arthritis	Kola: Fatigue	Motherwort: Urinary
Ginger: Motion Sickness	Larkspur: Lice	Mugwort: Liver Problems
Gingko: Memory, Alzheimers	Lavendar: Antidepressant	Muira-Puama: Impotemce
Ginseng: Immune Systrm	Lemon Balm: Tension	Mulberry: Adrenals
Goldenseal: Colitis	Licorice: Sore Throat	Muellin: Respiratory, Lymph
Gotu Kola: Immune System	Linden Flower: Hypertension	Myrrh: Pain, Gas
Gravelroot: Urinary	Lobelia: Asthma	Nettle: Anemia, Weakness
Hawthorne: Heart	Loquat: Hiccups	Oak Bark: Dysentery
Hop: Insomnia	Marjoram: Digestion	Oats: Depression
Horehound: Cough	Marshmallow: Colds	Oregano: Digestion, Immunity
Horsetail: Anti-Inflammatory	Mate: Stimulant	Papaya: Digestion
Hyssop: Colds, Flu	May Apple: Warts	Parsley: Diuretic, Bad Breath
Irish Moss: Dry Cough	Meadowsweet: Pain	Pau D'Arco: Autoimmune
Juniper: Gout, Gas	Milk Thistle: Liver, Hepatitis	Passionflower: Insomnia

HERB CHART 3

Herb/Uses	Herb/Uses	Herb/Uses
Pennyroyal: Nervous Tension	Sarsaparilla: Venereal Disease	Valerian: Insomnia
Plantain: Anti-Inflammatory	Savory: Coughs	Vervain: Liver Disorders
Poppy: Pain, Anxiety	Saw Palmetto: Prostate	Violet: Sore Throat
Psyillium: Constipation	Senna: Constipation	Walnut: Strength
Raspberry: Menstrual	Sheperds Purse: Bleeding	Wild Cherry: Ulcers
Red Clover: Cancer, Immune	Skullcap: Hiccoughs	Wild Yam: Gall Stones
Red Pepper: Headache	Skunk Cabbage: Nervousness	Willow: Analgesic
Rhubarb: Constipation	Slippery Elm: Throat, Ulcers	Witch Hazel: Discharge
Rose: Circulation	Speramint: Headaches	Wood Betony: Anxiety
Rose Hips: Colds, Flu	Suma: Energy	Wormwood: Hepatitis
Rosemary: Joint Inflammation	St Johns Wort: Depression, Aids	Yarrow: Hemorrhoids
Rue: Cramps, Spasms	Tansy: Convulsions	Yellow Dock: Anemia
Safflower: Kidney, Nerves	Tarragon: Antiseptic	Yerba Mate: Immune System
Saffron: High Cholesterol	Tea: High Cholesterol	Yerba Santa: Respiratory
Sage: Food Poisoning	Thyme: Coughs	Yucca: Arthritis, Joint Pain
Sarsaparilla: Venereal (VD)	Turmeric: Inflammation	Violet: Sore Throat
Sassafras: Arthritis	Uva Ursi: Urinary, Herpes	Walnut: Strength

I Ching

The I Ching or Book of Changes has been used for over 3,000 years. This philosophical system is based on quantum physics and mathematics. A Hexgram is a six line structure comprised of solid and broken lines. There are 64 Hexagrams. A Trigram is a three line structure made up of solid and broken lines. Two Trigrams make up a Hexagram. There are 8 Trigrams which have meanings and a cyclic Cycle. The ASCII computer software code is based on the I Ching. I encourage people who are interested to research more on this subject.

I CHING TRIGRAMS

Name	Trigram	Direction/ Animal	Emblem/ Element	Time of Day/Year	Body Part	Qualities
CH'IEN		Northwest/ Dragon Horse	Heaven/ Metal	Daytime/ Early Winter	Head	Creative Vitality Strength
CHEN		East/ Flying Dragon	Thunder/ Wood	Early Morning/ Spring	Foot	Activity Growth Arousing
K'AN		North/ Pig	Water, Moon/ Water	Midnight/ Mid-Winter	Ear	Mental Difficult Mysterious
KEN		Northeast/ Dog, Rat, Birds	Mountain/ Wood	Dawn/ Late Winter	Hand	Calm Still Waiting
K'UN		Southwest/ Mare, Ox	Earth/ Earth	Night/ Early Autumn	Belly	Receptive Adaptable Nourishing
SUN		Southeast/ Hen	Wind/ Wood	Mid-Morning/ Early Summer	Thigh	Honest Growth Gentle
LI		South/ Toad, Crab, Snail	Lightening/ Fire	Noon, Mid-Summer	Eye	Intelligent Conscious Illuminating
TUI		West/ Sheep	Lake/ Water, Metal	Twilight/ Late Autumn	Mouth	Pleasure Reflection Satisfaction

I CHING TRIGRAMS

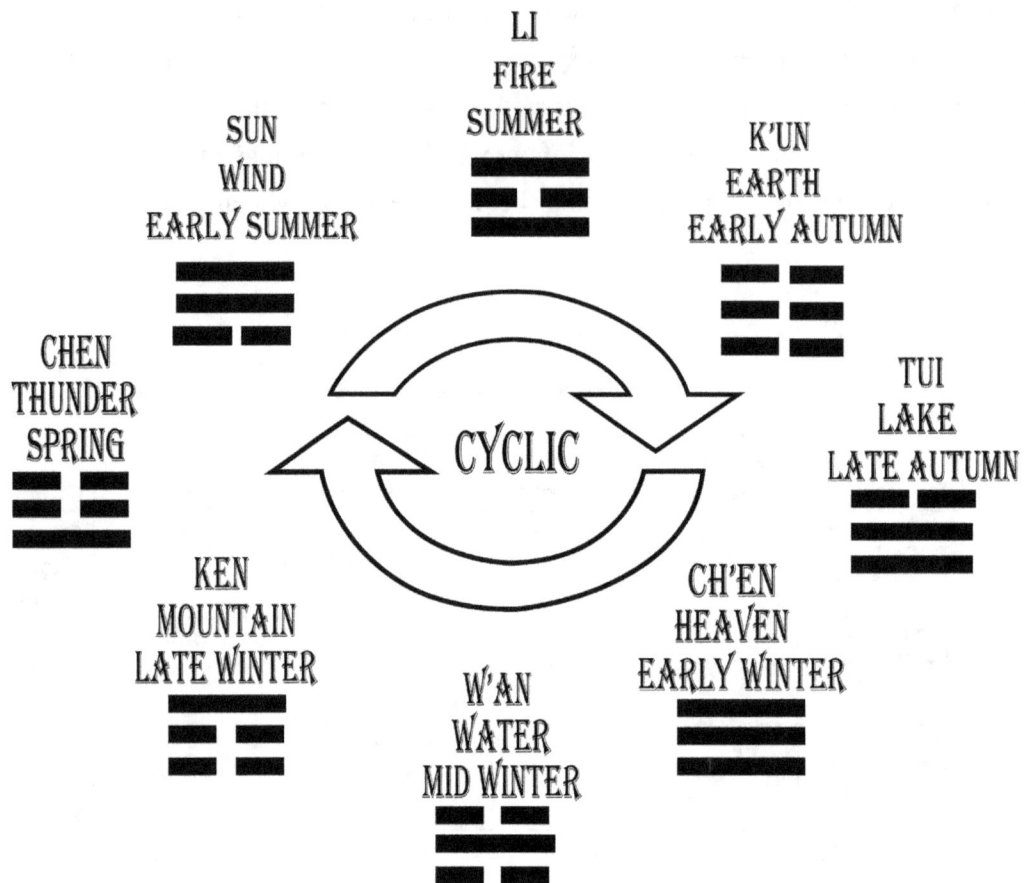

KING WEN TRIGRAM ARRANGEMENT

⚏ YIN - PASSIVE/YIELDING
⚌ YANG - STRONG/ACTIVE

I CHING FORTUNE: COIN TOSS

The I Ching takes a look at human behavior in relationships to the elements. Action or change is considered to affect individual action and the Universe. The I Ching, similar to an oracle, is a way to discover insights on how to align yourself with Universal principles to allow positive energy into your life and overcome obstacles. There are many different ways to consult the IChing. The coin toss method is a very old, proven method to provide you insight.

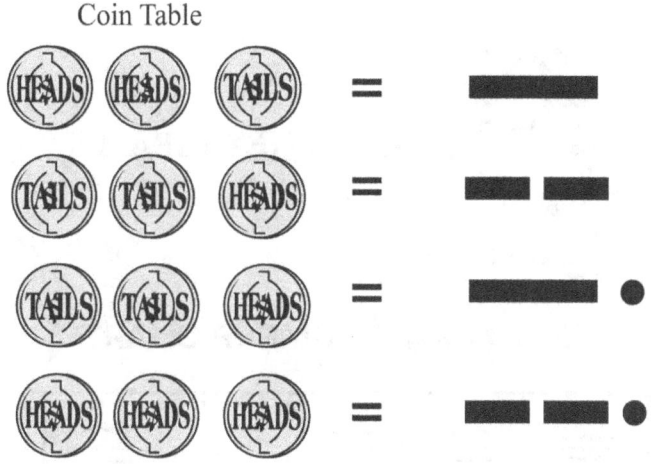

HEXAGRAM COIN TOSS METHOD

Write out your Question. Now think of your question and toss 3 coins 6 times. The 1st Toss represents the 6th line; the second toss the 5th line, etc. Draw the corresponding line from the coin table for each toss.

Go to the Hexagram Table and find your Hexagram number. Then look at the I Ching Fortune Telling Chart and read the message associated with your number to get the answer to your question. Please note: In the coin table if your coin toss has a dot after the line it represents a changing line. To get your answer create a reverse Hexagram and then look up both Hexagram numbers on the Fortune Telling Chart.

EXAMPLE OF A REVERSE HEXAGRAM

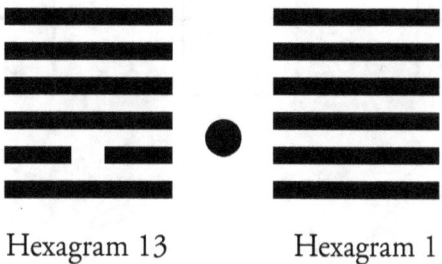

Hexagram 13   Hexagram 1

EXAMPLE OF FINDING HEXAGRAM NUMBER:

Your Coin Toss:

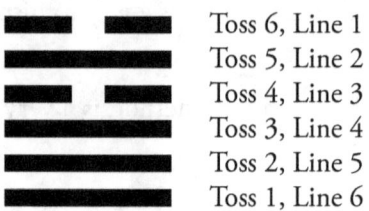

Toss 6, Line 1
Toss 5, Line 2
Toss 4, Line 3
Toss 3, Line 4
Toss 2, Line 5
Toss 1, Line 6

EXAMPLE: 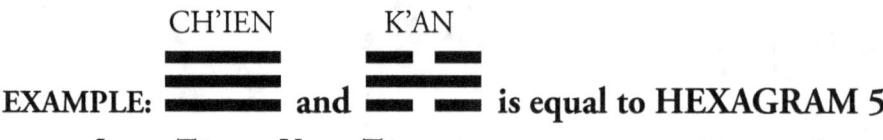 is equal to HEXAGRAM 5

Lower Trigram   Upper Trigram

HEXAGRAM NUMBER CHART

UPPER → LOWER ↓	CHIEN	CHEN	K'AN	KEN	K'UN	SUN	LI	TUI
CHIEN	1	34	5	26	11	9	14	43
CHEN	25	51	3	27	24	42	21	47
K'AN	6	40	29	4	7	59	64	47
KEN	33	62	39	52	15	53	56	31
K'UN	12	16	8	23	2	20	35	45
SUN	44	32	48	18	46	57	50	28
LI	13	55	63	22	36	37	30	49
TUI	10	54	60	41	19	61	38	58

I CHING FORTUNE TELLING CHART

#	Meaning	#	Meaning	#	Meaning	#	Meaning
1	Creative Power	17	Adapting	33	Retreat	49	Changing
2	Natural Response	18	Repair	34	Great Power	50	Cosmic Order
3	Difficult Beginnings	19	Promotion	35	Progress	51	Shocking
4	Inexperience	20	Contemplation	36	Censorship	52	Meditation
5	Calculated Waiting	21	Reform	37	Family	53	Developing
6	Conflict	22	Grace	38	Contradiction	54	Subordinate
7	Collective Force	23	Deterioration	39	Obstacles	55	Zenith
8	Unity	24	Repeating	40	Liberation	56	Traveling
9	Restrained	25	Innocence	41	Decline	57	Penetrating Influence
10	Conduct	26	Potential Energy	42	Benefit	58	Encouraging
11	Prospering	27	Nourishing	43	Resolution	59	Reuniting
12	Stagnation	28	Critical Mass	44	Temptation	60	Limitations
13	Community	29	Danger	45	Assembling	61	Insight
14	Sovereignty	30	Synergy	46	Advancement	62	Conscientiousness
15	Moderation	31	Attraction	47	Adversity	63	After the End
16	Harmony	32	Continuing	48	The Source	64	Before the End

Reflexology

Reflexology is where there is a belief that all parts of the body have a corresponding pressure point on the feet. By applying pressure or rubbing the feet in that specific area it is believed you can relieve symptoms from ailments and illnesses.

Reflexology is thousands of years old and was thought to have started in China. In 2330 B.C. one of the first written records was a picture in the tomb of the Egyptian Ankhamor. However reflexology was known and used by many ancient civilizations such as India and Sumeria. It was believed that Marco Polo introduced reflexology to Europe after translating a Chinese massage book into Italian in the 1300s. It was first written about in American around 1917.

Although people think reflexology is mostly about the feet, other parts of the body such as the hands, ear and face are also considered to have reflexology points.

Reflexologists are practitioners that access the reflexology points on the bottom, sides and top of the feet which is supposed to have an effect on the body's organs and the entire body systems.

It is said that reflexology may help: to reduce pain, stress and anxiety; improve mood and well-being; boosts the immune system; help recovery from back problems and hormone imbalances; improve digestion and fertility.

Reflexology is simple and effective and but there may be some instances where you might need to be cautious or avoid it all together. You should consult with your natural health practitioner, reflexologists or health provider prior to treatment if you are healing from a foot fracture, have vascular disease, gout or osteoarthritis, are pregnant, have blood clot issues or have open wounds.

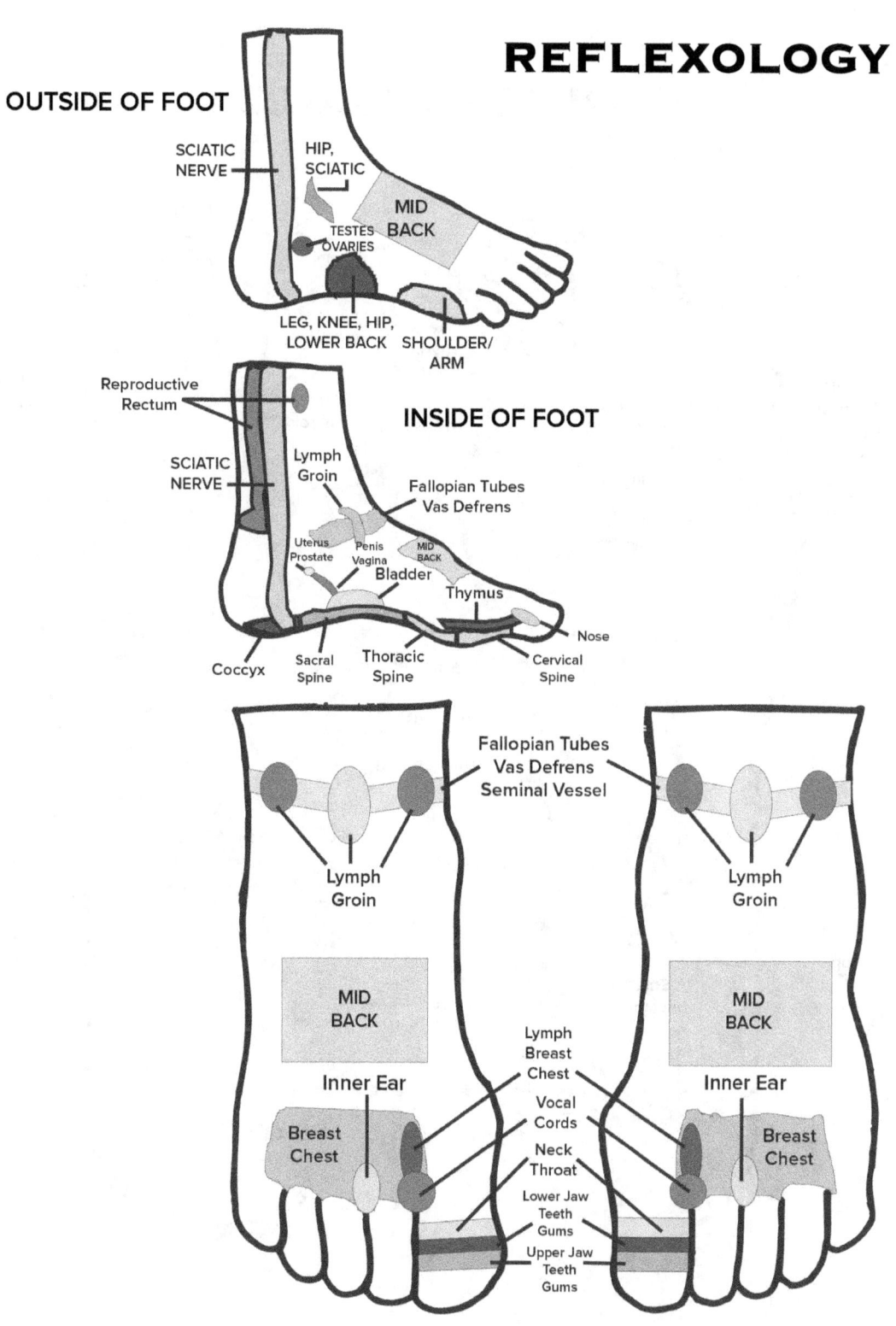

REFLEXOLOGY

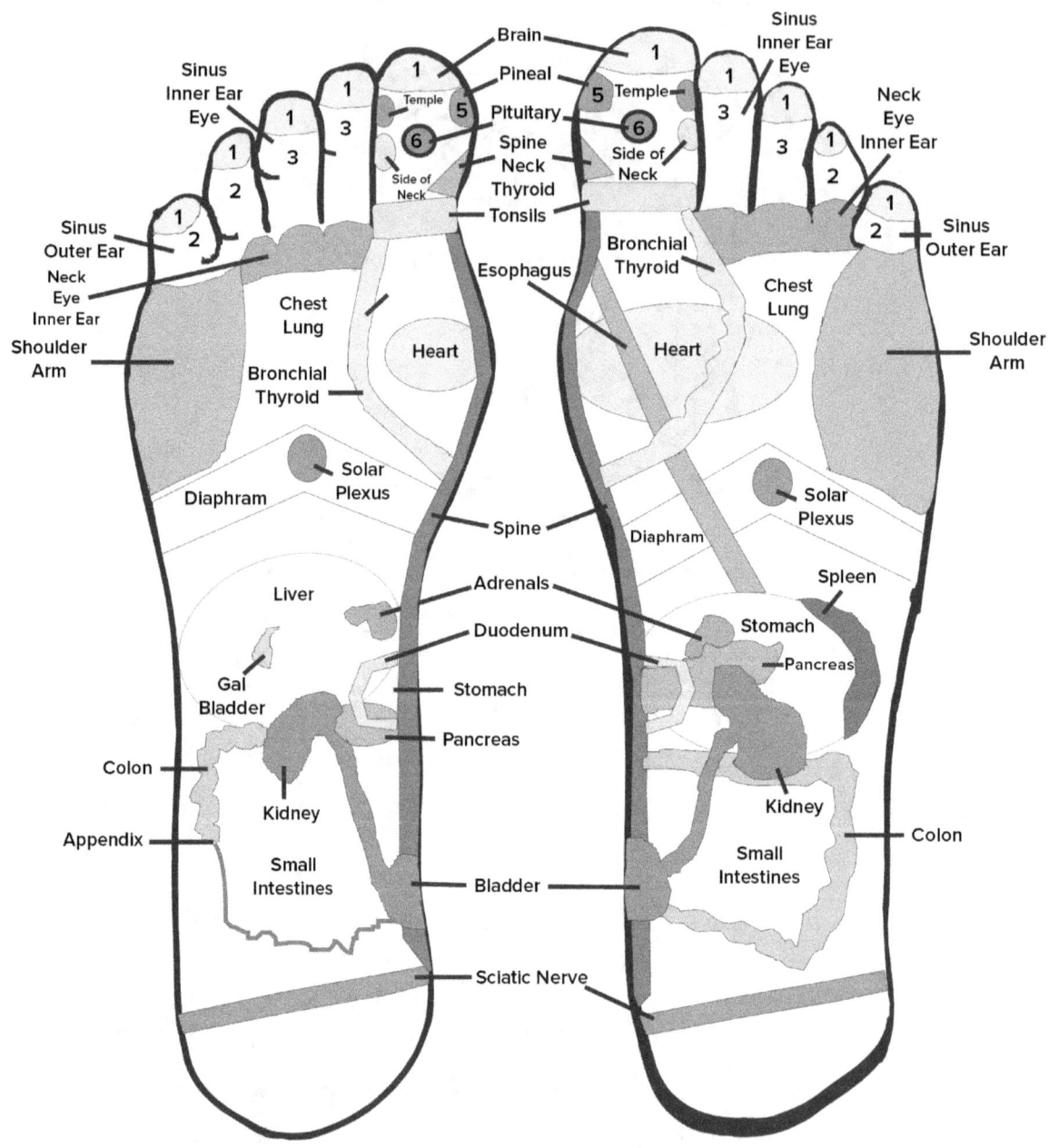

Runes

The "Father of the Runes" is considered to be the God Odin. The Vikings believed the Runes were created when Odin, trying to get secret knowledge, speared himself to the cosmic tree named Yggdrasil. It is said that the ancient Norse word 'rune' means secret knowledge.

Runes are the spiritual alphabet of the Ancient Northern European people. This Runic alphabet, known from the first century A.D., was called Futhark. The Elder Futhark is the oldest version. The Younger Futhark, the Runes used today, gradually evolved from the Elder Futhark Runic alphabet by the beginning of the Viking Age around 800 A.D.

There are 24 letters in the Futhark. Each rune letter has a specific symbol, a phonetic sound and meanings linked to Norse mythology. The Futhark was used for writing on stone, bone and wood as a means of communication. Regarded as sacred, the Runes were also used as a means for decision making, medical purposes, enlightenment, guidance and spell casting.

Runemasters, who held high positions in the Viking clans, were trained to use and understand the Runes which was part of everyday life.

Rune casting, was a method of divination that was done by Rune Casters who were mostly women. To answer the question that was asked, the Rune Caster would either select three runes from their sacred pouch, lay all the runes facedown and pick three or dump all the Runes out of the pouch and the Runes that landed face up were used for the reading.

How the Runes are selected from the pouch is important. If they are selected bottom up there are different meanings for these inverted Runes which are different from the ones selected right side up. Make no mistake Runes are very powerful. I encourage you to research the Runes further if you are inclined to work with them.

RUNE CHART

Sign	Key Word/ Symbol/Color	Gemstone/ God/Goddess	Element/ Firewood	Object/ Metal	Meaning
ᚠ FEOH	Possession/ Cattle		Fire		Dominion, Wealth, Luxury, Possession
ᚢ UR	Action/ Aurocha		Fire		Freedom, Courage, Strength, Action
ᚦ THORN	Evil/ Devil/ Grey	Opal/ Loki	Water/ Thorn	Shoes/ Arsenic	Envy, Cleansing, Nemesis, Purging
ᚩ OS	Good/ God/ White	Diamond/ Odin	Water/ Ash	Spear/ Mercury	Wisdom, Truth, Love, Health
ᚱ RAD	Journey/ Riding		Air		Travel, Evolution, Escape, Relocation
ᚲ KEN	Beacon/ Torch		Air		Revelation, Clarity, Vision, Knowledge,
ᚷ GYFU	Gift/ Gift		Earth		Gift, Request, Legacy, Offering
ᚹ WYN	Happiness/ Glory		Earth		Joy, Ecstasy, Legacy, Bliss
ᚺ HAEGL	Hardship/ Hail		Fire		Tempering, Testing, Trial Rebuilding
ᚾ NYD	Necessity/ Need		Fire		Necessity, Want, Need, Torment
ᛁ IS	Entrapment/ Ice/ Black	Jet/ Hel	Water/ Willow	Veil/ Lead	Glamour, Allure, Invitation, Infatuation
ᛃ GER	Change/ Harvest		Water		Change, Luck, Alteration, Fruition

RUNE CHART (cont.)

Sign	Key Word/ Symbol/Color	Gemstone/ God/Goddess	Element/ Firewood	Object/ Metal	Meaning
EOH	Duty/ Yew/ Blue	Sapphire/ Heimdall	Air/ Yew	Horn/ Steel	Truth, Reliable, Strength, Tenacity
PEROD	Pleasure/ Apple/ Green	Emerald/ Frija	Air/ Apple	Necklace/ Copper	Abundance, Sensuality, Luxury, Opulence
EOLH	Protection/ Defense		Earth		Protection, Shield, Defense, Guardian
SIGEL	Retribution/ Sun/ Orange	Jasper/ Thor	Earth/ Oak	Hammer/ Tin	Power, Energy, Act of Will, Force
TYR	Judgement/ Tiw/ Red	Ruby/ Tiw	Fire/ Fir	Sword/ Iron	Victory, Valor, Honor, Integrity
BEORC	Fertility/ Birch/ Purple	Amethyst/ Freyja	Fire/ Birch	Cloak/ Silver	Love, Growth, Healing, Fertility
EH	Transformation/ Horse		Water		Grace, Speed, Movement, Transportation
MAN	Intelligence/ Man		Water		Invention, Ability, Intelligence, Skill
LAGU	Unconscious/ Water		Air		Mystery, History, Dreams, Fantasies
ING	Growth/ Fertility		Air		Stability, Caring, Family, Good Sense
DAEG	Completion/ Day/ Yellow	Topaz/ Balder	Earth/ Mistletoe	Bow/ Gold	Rebirth, Cycle, Period, Phase
ETHEL	Home/ Homeland/ Red Brown	Agate/ Frey	Earth/ Pine	Chariot/ Bronze	Patriotism, Karma, Home, Property

Sioux Four Directions

The energy directions of life are located in the four Directions. The Four Directions are used anytime the Sioux do anything sacred. Each direction have meanings that raise awareness, provide power and facilitate growth.

These directions are also encompassed in the Medicine Wheel. We walked this wheel in all our stages of life. Each direction has a special meaning and different qualities and attributes. The cross symbolizes all directions.

The East signifies the Wisdom and Understanding. Ay dawn people face the East and pray for Wisdom and Understanding The South stands for warmth and growth. The West is vital because it stands for Water and nothing lives without water. The North stands for cleansing through the trials and discomfort that mankind must go through

SIOUX FOUR DIRECTIONS CHART

Direction	Life Stage	House	Color	Animal	Relation
EAST	Old Age Death Afterlife	Morning Star	Yellow	Dove Golden Eagle	Wisdom Understanding
SOUTH	Birth	Animal Spirits	White	Deer White Crane	Life Destiny
WEST	Youth	Thunder	Black	Buffalo Black Eagle	Purifying Water
NORTH	Middle Age	Calf Pipe Woman	Red	Bald Eagle	Health

SIOUX FOUR DIRECTIONS

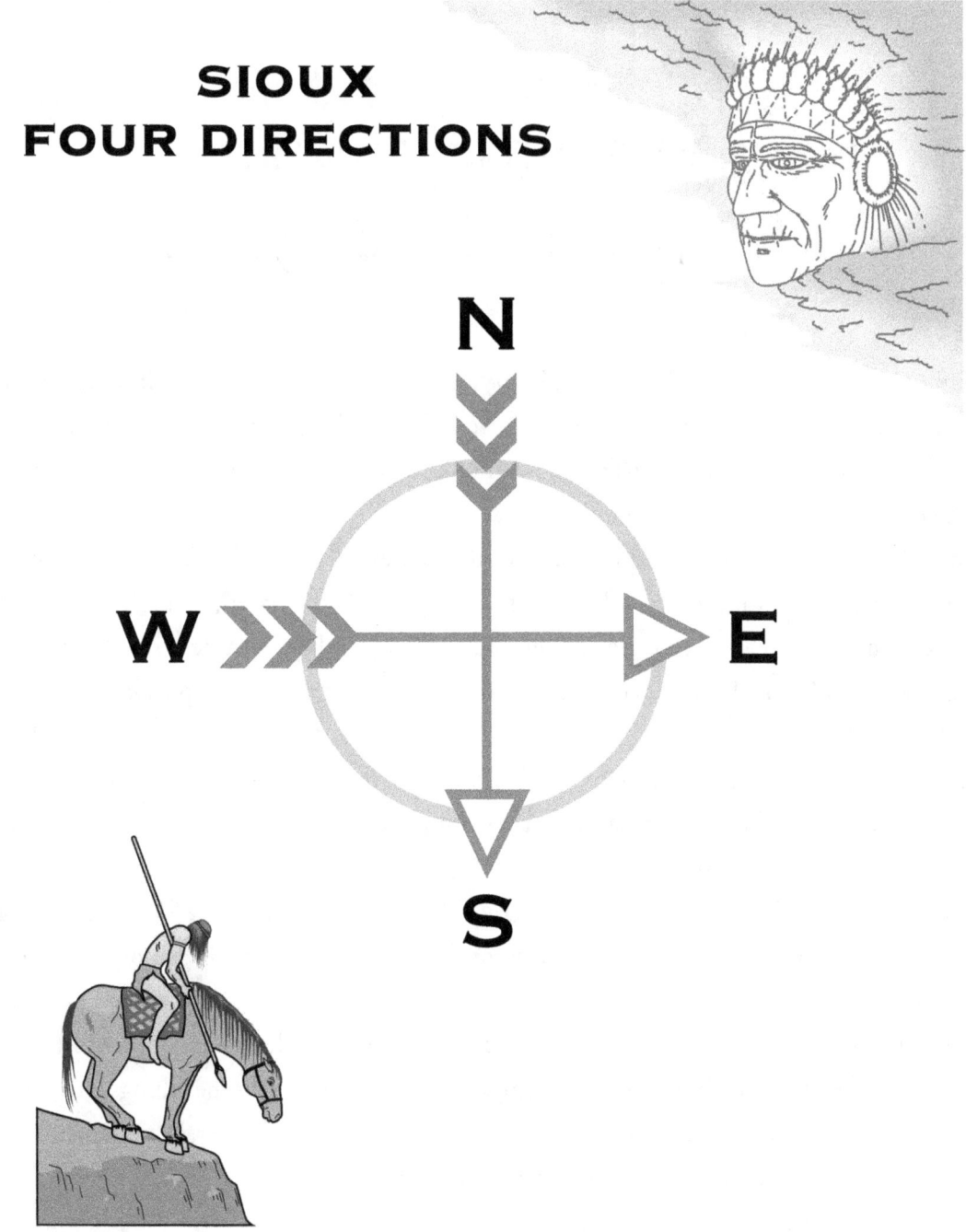

Vitamins, Minerals, Supplements, Enzymes

Vitamin, Minerals, dietary supplements and enzymes are important to maintain a healthy body. These days we do not get enough of our vital nutrients from food and supplementation can help keep the body healthy. Every body is different so make sure you talk to your natural health care practitioner or do the research yourself to find what may be right for you.

Vitamins are micronutrients and co-enzymes that are essential to life. Vitamins are involved metabolism, and the biochemical processes that release energy. There are water-soluble vitamins that the body cannot store and need to be taken daily and oil soluble vitamins that are stored in fatty tissue and the liver for longer periods of time. Examples of water soluble vitamins are: C, B complex. Examples of oil soluble vitamins are: A, D, E.

Amino Acids are made up of proteins and are known as the building blocks of life. Proteins are necessary for every cell in the body. There are about 28 amino acids that are combined to create the hundreds of proteins that the body needs for life.

Dietary or Whole Food Supplements are derived from the byproducts of food that are high in nutrients or have active ingredients to aid metabolism or digestion. Examples are: acidolphilus, bee pollen and bee propolis.

Bulk minerals (macrominerals) are needed in larger amounts than trace minerals (microminerals). Minerals are primarily stored in the bone and muscle tissue and, among other things, are basically needed to maintain chemical balance of the body's systems. Examples of bulk minerals are: calcium, magnesium. Examples of trace minerals are: copper, iron, zinc, chromium.

Enzymes – are called the sparks of life because they are energized protein molecules that are needed for food digestion, brain stimulation, cellular energy and repair. Examples are amylase, cellulase, lipase, protease and lactase.

Here is some information on selecting supplements. Do choose a supplement that is a natural color. Most Red, Blue or Purple supplements contain artificial dyes or colorings. Do not choose supplements with synthetic vitamin C & E. There are differences in functions, breakdown and absorption. The best natural source of Vitamin E are mixed d-tocopherols (not dl-tocopherols) and natural sources for vitamin C are rose hips and calcium ascorbate. Avoid supplements with sugar, starch, corn, wheat, iron,

~ VITAMINS, MINERALS, SUPPLEMENTS, ENZYMES ~

dairy, salt, artificial flavorings, artificial sweeteners or artificial preservatives. Do not chose a supplement based on price. Some high end vitamins are not necessarily using better ingredients. With most low priced supplements you may not be getting the potency you need, or they may be using synthetics ingredients or a high amount of fillers such as cellulose to keep the price low. Do not assume that by buying a name brand that you are getting quality so do your research but make sure you buy from a reputable manufacturer. Do try to find a basic multi-supplement that includes all the vitamins, minerals, bioflavinoids, enzymes, natural food concentrates, antioxidants, herbs, essential fatty acids, fiber and green foods in one formula. This will keep the amount of pills you are taking to a minimum and will also be better for your budget. Do buy a vitamin with all the B's in it because all the B's work synergistically together. Do remember that on a label the "other ingredients" are listed in order of potency. So if you see fillers like cellulose, before the actual supplement name then you are getting more fillers than supplement. Also please remember it will usually take a 4-6 week period before you see the effect of any supplement. The following charts are a general overview and for more detailed information please do your own research or ask your health care practitioner.

VITAMIN, MINERAL SUPPLEMENT CHART 1

Name	Activity	Uses
A Beta Carotene	New Cell growth. Fights Infection. Antioxidant.	Essential for skin, bones and blood.
B1 Thiamine	Metabolizes Sugar and Salt. Aids Nervous System.	Large amount aids diabetes and small amount aids hypoglycemia.
B2 Riboflavin	Good Muscle Tone. Metabolism of Fat, Protein and Carbohydrates.	Important for visions, skin, hair and nails.
B3 Niacin	Nervous and Digestive Systems.	Healthy Skin
B5 Pantothenic Acid	Energy, Hormone and Antibody Production.	Strengthens adrenal activity.
B6 Pyrodoxine	Energy Production. Utilizes Fats and Proteins.	Large amount aids diabetes.
B12 Cyanocobalamin	Builds Blood. Aids Brain and Nervous System.	Aids Stress and large amounts helps hypoglycemia.
Bee Pollen	Antimicrobial. Strengthens the Immune System.	Aids fatigue, depression, cancer and colon disorders.
Biotin	Produces Energy. Metabolizes Fats.	Forms RNA, DNA and synthesizes amino acids.
C Ascorbic Acid	Antioxidant,. Antibacterial. Collagen and Red Blood Cell Production. Aids Clotting.	Aids clotting, immune system, blood cells, cholesterol.
Calcium	Strong Bones and Teeth. Essential for Heart Rhythm.	Aids clotting, thyroid, adrenals and calms nerves.
Choline	Neurotransmitter. Aids Kidneys and Bladder.	Aids nerve fibers, slows fast pulse rate and aids digestion.
Chromium	Glucose Metabolism. Synthesizes Fatty Acids and Cholesterol	Large amounts help diabetes small amounts helps hypoglycemia.
CoQ10 Ubiquinone	Immune System, Energy, Cell Oxygen Level.	Helps the overweight. Aids tissue healing, angina, hypertension, vascular disease.
Copper	Aids Hemoglobin, Red Blood Cells, Bone Formation and Adrenal Function.	Thyroid, Hormones, Calcium Utilization, Arthritis, Joint Pain
D Calciferol	Aids Weak Muscles, Immune System. Utilizes Calcium and Phosphorus.	Antiviral. Large amount aids diabetes and small amount aids Hypoglycemia.
DMG N-Dimethylglycine	Reduces Seizures. Aids Glucose Levels, Liver Function, Increases B and T Lymphocytes.	Antiviral. Detoxifier. Antioxidant. Increases Interferon.

~ VITAMINS, MINERALS, SUPPLEMENTS, ENZYMES ~

VITAMIN, MINERAL SUPPLEMENT CHART 2

Name	Activity	Uses
E Mixed Tocopherols	Antioxidant. Provides Oxygen to Muscles. Protects Hormone Membranes.	Prolongs red blood cell life. Aids blood clotting.
Evening Primrose Oil	Essential Fatty Acid. Aids Hormone Production.	Aids proper organ function.
Folic Acid	Synthesizes Nucleic Proteins (e.g., RNA, DNA).	Needed for red blood cells.
Garlic	Helps Immune System, Antibacterial.	Reduces blood pressure and fights infection.
Germanium GE132	Aids Cell Function and efficient oxygen. Antioxidant.	Anti-Arthritic. Anti-tumor. Antiviral.
L-Cysteine	Aids Immune System. Antibacterial. Antiviral.	Helps wound healing. Aids chelation of heavy metals.
L-Glutamine Amino Acid	High Level Brain Activity Source.	Lessens mental fatigue.
L-Lysine	Antiviral. Builds Antibodies.	Build new tissue, Aids hormones and cold sores.
L-Phenylalaine	Decreases Pain. Antidepressant. Stimulates the Pituitary gland.	Aids endorphin production.
Inositol	Fat Metabolism. Hair Growth.	Brain cell nutrient.
Iron Ferrous Sulphate	Hemoglobin Production.	Large amount aids diabetes and small amount aids Hypoglycemia.
Lecithin	Aids Digestion and Cholesterol.	Helps prevent infection, gall stones and fatty liver.
Magnesium	Nerve Function and Heart Rhythm.	Bone and heart maintenance.
Manganese	Protein and Fat Utilization. Maintains Nervous System.	Aids sex hormone production.
MAX EPA	Cell Membrane Formation. Lowers Cholesterol.	Used by brain nerve Fibers.

VITAMIN, MINERAL SUPPLEMENT CHART 3

Name	Activity	Uses
PABA	Forms Red Blood Cells. Utilization of Fats and Carbohydrates.	Hair Pigmentation.
Phosphorus	Cell Maintenance.	Aids nerve conduction.
Potassium	Heart Rhythm. Nerve Conduction.	Balances minerals in the blood.`
Selenium	Antioxidant.	Aids body growth and metabolism.
SOD complex Superoxide, Catalase, Glutathione, Peroxidase	Neutralizes Free Radicals. Aids in Radiation protection.	Lessens emotional, physical and nutritional stress.
Tryptophane Amino Acid	Necessary for production of Vitamin B3, Produces serotonin.	Neurotransmitter responsible for normal sleep. Helps depression.
Tyrosine Amino Acid	Precursor to a adrenaline. Regulates Mood. Aids Melatonin Production. Aids active thyroid hormones.	Aids neurotransmitter dopamine and norepinephrine. Used for stress reduction and chronic fatigue,
Zinc	Necessary for Healing and Normal Growth. Aids New Cell Development.	Helps immune system, cold, flu and normal function of prostate gland,

ENZYME CHART

Name	Breaks Down
Amylase	Carbohydrates
Bromelain	Proteins
Cellulase	Fiber
Chyropapain	Proteins
Diastase	Carbohydrates
Lactase/Lactose	Milk and Sugar
Lipase	Fats
Maltase	Carbohydrates
Pancreatin	Proteins, fats, carbohydrates
Papain	Proteins, fats, carbohydrates
Rennin	Proteins
Trypsin	Proteins

Western Elements

Elements are the forces of Nature that can be expressed as a primary influence on the life force. The theory of the four element theory is said to have been started by the Greek philosopher, Empedocles around 440 B.C. and was later explained in detail by Aristotle. It is said that all of nature consists of these four elements: fire, air, earth and water. Aristotle added a fifth element of an unseen force called Ether and the Chinese added metal as their 5th element.

Each person or living being contains all of the elements in various arrangements but one is usually predominant. That one dominant element becomes the unique energetic structure of the individual. The four Western Elements have specific qualities, aspects and associations. The Western Element theory is infused into science, medical practices among many other things.

WESTERN ELEMENTS CHART

Element	Direction/ Numbers	Planets	Motivation /Tree	Color	Qualities
FIRE	South/ 1, 3, 4, 9	Mars Jupiter Son	Inspiration/ Almond	Red Orange Gold	Zeal, Courage, Creativity
EARTH	North/ 5, 6, 8	Venus Saturn	Physical/ Oak	White Brown Green Black	Nature, Dependable, Cautious
AIR	East/ 4, 5, 6	Mercury Venus Uranus	Mental/ Aspen	Yellow Red White	Curious, Logical, Perceptive
WATER	West/ 2, 3, 7, 9	Moon Pluto Neptune	Emotional/ Willow	Green Grey Blue	Psychic, Sensitive, Receptive

WESTERN ELEMENTS

Fill-In Charts

MY PERSONAL SYMBOLS

NAME: _____ **DATE**: _____

ANGEL SYMBOLS:

Hierarchy 1

Choir 1_____ Choir 2 _____ Choir 3 _____

Hierarchy 2

Choir 1_____ Choir 2 _____ Choir 3 _____

Hierarchy 3

Choir 1_____ Choir 2 _____ Choir 3 _____

Zodiac Angel _____ Month Angel _____

Day Archangel _____ Day Angel _____

Element Angel _____ Special Angel _____

ANIMAL SYMBOLS:

Animal 1 _____ Animal 2 _____ Spirit Guide _____

ARCHETYPE SYMBOL:

Myth or Archetype Name _____ Purpose _____

AROMATHERAPY OIL:

1st Favorite _____ 2nd Favorite _____ 3rd Favorite _____

~ SYMBOLS OF YOU ~

ASTROLOGY:

Sign _____ Motto _____ Symbol _____

Element _____ Planet _____ Colors _____

Gemstones _____ Body Part _____

Musical Note _____ Number _____ Archetype _____

Compatibility _____

AURA COLORS:

Colors _____

BACH FLOWERS:

Symptom _____ Remedy _____

Symptom _____ Remedy _____

BIRD SYMBOLS:

Bird 1 _____ Bird 2 _____ Spirit Guide _____

CANDLE COLORS:

Candle 1 _____ Purpose: _____

Candle 2 _____ Purpose: _____

Candle Color _____ Aromatherapy Scent _____ Purpose: _____

CHAKRAS:

Health Purpose: _____ Chakra(s) Effected: _____

Musical Note: _____ Color: _____ Gemstone: _____ Sound: _____

Emotional Purpose: _____ Chakra(s) Effected: _____

Musical Note: _____ Color: _____ Gemstone: _____ Sound: _____

Spiritual Purpose: _____ Chakra(s) Effected: _____

Musical Note: _____ Color: _____ Gemstone: _____ Sound: _____

~ FILL-IN CHARTS ~

COLORS:

Personality Color: _____ Favorite Color 1: _____ Favorite Color 2: _____

Health Purpose: _____ Healing Color: _____

Activates: _____ Used For: _____ Trigger Points: _____

CRYSTAL SYMBOLS:

Crystal 1 _____ Spiritual: _____

Crystal 2 _____ Physical: _____

Crystal 3 _____ Emotional: _____

FISH SYMBOLS:

Fish 1 _____ Hidden Potential: _____

Fish 2 _____ Personality Traits: _____

Fish 3 _____ Personality Traits: _____

Fish 4 _____ Personality Traits: _____

FLOWER SYMBOLS:

Flower 1 _____ Meaning: _____

Flower 2 _____ Meaning: _____

Flower 3 _____ Meaning: _____

GOD & GODDESS SYMBOLS:

Ancient God: _____ Meaning: _____

Ancient Goddess: _____ Meaning: _____

Goddess Sub-Symbol: _____ Meaning: _____

Zodiac Goddess: _____ Meaning: _____

NATIVE AMERICAN ANIMAL SPIRIT GUIDE:

My Native American Animal Spirit Guide 1: _____

My Native American Animal Spirit Guide 2: _____

~ SYMBOLS OF YOU ~

NUMBERS:

Favorite Number: _____ Meaning: _____

Lucky Number: _____ Meaning: _____

Spirit Path Number: _____ Meaning: _____

NUMEROLOGY:

Life Cycle Number: _____ Life Balance Number: _____ Life Destiny Number: _____

ORIENTAL HOROSCOPE:

Sign _____ Qualities _____

Best Love Match _____

Best To Avoid _____ Element _____

Planet _____ Yin/Yang _____

PALM READING:

Shape Hand _____ Meaning _____

Line Traits _____ Attributes _____

Line Color _____ Attributes _____

Mounts _____ Attributes _____

Markings _____ Attributes _____

PHRENOLOGY:

Intellect Bump # _____ Meaning _____

Sympathies Bump # _____ Meaning _____

Survival Bump # _____ Meaning _____

Ambitions Bump # _____ Meaning _____

Energy Bump # _____ Meaning _____

Emotions Bump # _____ Meaning _____

Social Instinct Bump # _____ Meaning _____

~ FILL-IN CHARTS ~

PLANETS:

Your Zodiac Sign: _____ Draw Your Planet's Symbol: _____

Your Planet: _____ Your Planet's Musical Note: _____

Planet Number: _____ Astrology House: _____

Element: _____ Polarity: _____

Sephirah: _____ Planet Rules: _____

Metal: _____ Gemstone: _____

PLAYING CARDS:

Your Birthday Playing Card: _____

Birthday Playing Date Card Meanings: _____

SHAPES, GEOMETRIC:

Your Key Geometric Shape: _____

Key Geometric Shape: _____

TAROT:

Your Key Tarot Card : _____

Key Tarot Card Meaning _____

TEA LEAF READING :

Your Personal Tea Leaf Shape: _____ Meaning: _____

TREES:

Your Personal Power Tree: _____ Meaning: _____

WATER:

Your Personal Power Tree: _____ Meaning: _____

~ FILL-IN CHARTS ~

~ SYMBOLS OF YOU ~

MY PERSONAL SYMBOLS

NAME: _____ **DATE:** _____

ANGEL SYMBOLS:

Hierarchy 1

Choir 1 _____ Choir 2 _____ Choir 3 _____

Hierarchy 2

Choir 1 _____ Choir 2 _____ Choir 3 _____

Hierarchy 3

Choir 1 _____ Choir 2 _____ Choir 3 _____

Zodiac Angel _____ Month Angel _____

Day Archangel _____ Day Angel _____

Element Angel _____ Special Angel _____

ANIMAL SYMBOLS:

Animal 1 _____ Animal 2 _____ Spirit Guide _____

ARCHETYPE SYMBOL:

Myth or Archetype Name _____ Purpose _____

AROMATHERAPY OIL:

1st Favorite _____ 2nd Favorite _____ 3rd Favorite _____

ASTROLOGY:

Sign _____ Motto _____ Symbol _____

Element _____ Planet _____ Colors _____

Gemstones _____ Body Part _____

Musical Note _____ Number _____ Archetype _____

Compatibility _____

~ FILL-IN CHARTS ~

AURA COLORS:

Colors _____

BACH FLOWERS:

Symptom _____ Remedy _____

Symptom _____ Remedy _____

BIRD SYMBOLS:

Bird 1 _____ Bird 2 _____ Spirit Guide _____

CANDLE COLORS:

Candle 1 _____ Purpose: _____

Candle 2 _____ Purpose: _____

Candle Color _____ Aromatherapy Scent _____ Purpose: _____

CHAKRAS:

Health Purpose: _____ Chakra(s) Effected: _____

Musical Note: _____ Color: _____ Gemstone: _____ Sound: _____

Emotional Purpose: _____ Chakra(s) Effected: _____

Musical Note: _____ Color: _____ Gemstone: _____ Sound: _____

Spiritual Purpose: _____ Chakra(s) Effected: _____

Musical Note: _____ Color: _____ Gemstone: _____ Sound: _____

COLORS:

Personality Color: _____ Favorite Color 1: _____ Favorite Color 2: _____

Health Purpose: _____ Healing Color: _____

Activates: _____ Used For: _____ Trigger Points: _____

~ SYMBOLS OF YOU ~

CRYSTAL SYMBOLS:

Crystal 1 _____   Spiritual: _____

Crystal 2 _____   Physical: _____

Crystal 3 _____   Emotional: _____

FISH SYMBOLS:

Fish 1 _____   Hidden Potential: _____

Fish 2 _____   Personality Traits: _____

Fish 3 _____   Personality Traits: _____

Fish 4 _____   Personality Traits: _____

FLOWER SYMBOLS:

Flower 1 _____   Meaning: _____

Flower 2 _____   Meaning: _____

Flower 3 _____   Meaning: _____

GOD & GODDESS SYMBOLS:

Ancient God: _____   Meaning: _____

Ancient Goddess: _____   Meaning: _____

Goddess Sub-Symbol: _____   Meaning: _____

Zodiac Goddess: _____   Meaning: _____

NATIVE AMERICAN ANIMAL SPIRIT GUIDE:

My Native American Animal Spirit Guide 1: _____

My Native American Animal Spirit Guide 2: _____

~ FILL-IN CHARTS ~

NUMBERS:

Favorite Number: _____ Meaning: _____

Lucky Number: _____ Meaning: _____

Spirit Path Number: _____ Meaning: _____

NUMEROLOGY:

Life Cycle Number: _____ Life Balance Number: _____ Life Destiny Number: _____

ORIENTAL HOROSCOPE:

Sign _____ Qualities _____

Best Love Match _____

Best To Avoid _____ Element _____

Planet _____ Yin/Yang _____

PALM READING:

Shape Hand _____ Meaning _____

Line Traits _____ Attributes _____

Line Color _____ Attributes _____

Mounts _____ Attributes _____

Markings _____ Attributes _____

PHRENOLOGY:

Intellect Bump # _____ Meaning _____

Sympathies Bump # _____ Meaning _____

Survival Bump # _____ Meaning _____

Ambitions Bump # _____ Meaning _____

Energy Bump # _____ Meaning _____

Emotions Bump # _____ Meaning _____

Social Instinct Bump # _____ Meaning _____

~ SYMBOLS OF YOU ~

PLANETS:

Your Zodiac Sign: _____ Draw Your Planet 's Symbol: _____

Your Planet: _____ Your Planet's Musical Note: _____

Planet Number: _____ Astrology House: _____

Element: _____ Polarity: _____

Sephirah: _____ Planet Rules: _____

Metal: _____ Gemstone: _____

PLAYING CARDS:

Your Birthday Playing Card: _____

Birthday Playing Date Card Meanings: _____

SHAPES, GEOMETRIC:

Your Key Geometric Shape: _____

Key Geometric Shape: _____

TAROT:

Your Key Tarot Card : _____

Key Tarot Card Meaning _____

TEA LEAF READING:

Your Personal Tea Leaf Shape: _____ Meaning: _____

TREES:

Your Personal Power Tree: _____ Meaning: _____

WATER:

Your Personal Power Tree: _____ Meaning: _____

~ SYMBOLS OF YOU ~

ramcontent.com/pod-product-compliance
g Source LLC
e TN
61936070526
9LV00060B/3842